IMPLEMENTING PROJECTS

IMPLEMENTING PROJECTS
A Manager's Guide

Trevor L. Young

The Industrial Society

First published in 1993 by
The Industrial Society
Robert Hyde House
48 Bryanston Square
London W1H 7LN
Telephone: 0171-479 2000

© *The Industrial Society 1993*
Reprinted October 1996
Reprinted August 1997
Reprinted March 1998

ISBN 0 85290 880 6

British Library Cataloguing-in-Publication Data.
A catalogue record for this book is available from the
British Library.

The Industrial Society is a Registered Charity No. 290003

Typeset by: The Midlands Book Typesetting Company
Printed by: Galliard (Printers) Ltd, Great Yarmouth
Cover design: Rhodes Design

Author's Note

The implementation and execution of a project is a natural progression from the planning phase. The same is true for this book which is designed to help you prepare and effectively carry out the work of a project when the primary planning is complete. The planning of a project has been examined in detail in **Planning Projects*** with an example project and the derivation of the essential documentation to help you evolve an effective plan.

In drafting the contents and layout of this book I have presumed that you are familiar with the **Twenty Steps to Effective Planning**. This has been deliberate and unavoidable since the all the phases of any project are intimately inter-related and inter-dependent. **Implementing Projects** by necessity, refers to the example project and the docu-

*For details see Appendix 3

mentation developed to record your plan in detail. Consequently I earnestly recommend that you read the earlier book dedicated to the planning process.

The glossary of terms in common use in project management is included again in Appendix 2. This has been extended to include terms that appear in this book.

T. L. Young

Contents

List of Figures

Introduction

This book is about the execution of projects – and that is not about entering the 'killing zone'. You have spent a considerable amount of effort in preparing for the moment when you can hit the 'go' button, then sit back in relative leisure and watch it all happen! Unfortunately this is mere fantasy if you have believed this is how things will proceed from now.

You have been engaged in the planning process, attempting to gather as much relevant information as possible to enable you to establish a clear plan for your project. You have already met numerous difficulties in this process and take pride in your success in overcoming everything that has blocked your progress up to now. Before entering the next phase of the project it is valid to take a step back, overview the current status of the project, and evaluate what has happened this far.

Review the contents of your **Project Diary** – if you do not have one, now is the time to start. Use a hard-backed lined notebook, preferably A4 size, where you can record everything that happens on the project from now. Remind yourself who has co-operated well with you, particularly in the stakeholder list you derived at the start of the project. Identify where you anticipate problems in the future, amongst senior management, the line management and others. This prepares you for the negotiations and discussions you must have to **organise the project** for a successful implementation. Your control of the project in this next phase is very dependent on inter-personal relationships and it is appropriate to prepare yourself by identifying where and with whom you have to work extra hard to achieve the desired results. The **control system** you now establish is one of the ways you can ensure you maintain this control at all times.

Of course everyone else apparently knows better than you, especially those who have had little or no involvement with the project up to this point. Such people are always ready to tell you their views even though they do not have all the facts. Additionally if there are any hidden feelings of envy or rivalry there is scope for some form of sabotage to prevent your achieving your objectives. This may quite simply take the form of poor co-operation or people rearranging work priorities for their staff without informing you. You continue to believe project work is continuing on track when in fact the opposite is the reality.

There is really minimal scope for supporting individual egos in project work unless the outcomes contribute directly to project success. Everything you have done until now and all your actions from this point are concerned primarily with what is best for the project. You must direct yourself – and your team if you have one – towards the project objectives without exception, since these reflect the agreed corporate needs. Your role as project leader is to create the enabling atmosphere to achieve the desired results.

At the final reckoning you are accountable to the project sponsor and the other key stakeholders for the success of the project, and responsible for the performance of yourself and your team throughout. The team will expect you to perform effectively as the project leader, and also give them the recognition and credit for their contribution to that success.

As you move into the execution phase of the project you are going to exercise all your skills, both technical and people management, to drive the project to the successful completion you seek. There are few projects that are truly confined in all their aspects to one department. Even if you are managing your project alone with no direct team, you are almost certainly going to request that certain parts of the work are executed by other specialist functional areas of the organisation. In practice this may be unavoidable, particularly with financial reporting and computing functions. In these situations it is appropriate to seek agreement that you have a **departmental representative** as a co-opted team member for as long as required. You can then direct all contact with these departments through the same individual. This helps you to maintain control of your project.

So executing projects involves many skills. Some of the more important of these are discussed in the following sections.

1

Preparing to Implement

You have reached the point where all your basic planning is complete and you are satisfied that all the essential elements of the work have been identified. If you have completed the essential steps of the planning process you now have this base plan presented in a documented form that is readily understood by everyone involved. This takes the form of the following documentation:

- An **OBJECTIVES** statement
- A **SCOPE OF WORK** statement
- A list or book of **SPECIFICATIONS** if appropriate
- A list of STAKEHOLDERS **with valuations**
- **A LOGIC DIAGRAM** for the **KEY STAGES**
- A **WORK BREAKDOWN STRUCTURE** for at least the **KEY STAGES**

- The **MILESTONE** schedule
- Clearly identified **SUCCESS FACTORS** and their method of measurement
- The **BAR CHART** for the **KEY STAGES** . . . . or
- A **NETWORK DIAGRAM** and **GANTT CHART** for the **KEY STAGES**
- A **LINEAR RESPONSIBILITY CHART** for the **KEY STAGES**
- An **APPROVED BUDGET** statement . . . . . . and
- An initial **OPERATING BUDGET** statement

At each step of the planning process to produce these documents you have taken particular care to ensure that the results derived are acceptable to the **key stakeholders**. This acceptance and approval is important to the effective implementation of the project. You need to be in a position where there is no doubt or uncertainty in the minds of the stakeholders or the project team about what is to be achieved or how you propose to carry out the necessary work. It is good practice if you can get all your plans to date 'signed off' as approved as this builds a stronger commitment by everyone involved. This is often the responsibility of the project Sponsor on behalf of all the key stakeholders.

You are now concerned to implement the project work, since this is the proof that all your efforts in planning are justified. However there are two further aspects of project management that you must stop and consider before you can enter the execution phase of the project:

- Derive a control system
- Organise the project work

Both are essential factors that make a significant contribution to project success.

The project control system

You know from the experience of planning your project up to this point that the process is re-iterative. There is really no such thing as the perfect plan, only an approach towards the best plan based on the available information at the time. As this information input is always open to change and renewal even the most detailed plans can suffer from a real need to be modified at intervals. It is a rare project that can be executed completely without any changes to the initial plans, for an abundance of reasons. This leads to the need for a mechanism to ensure that you can quickly react to changes when appropriate and get them accepted and signed off by the stakeholders.

Changes in corporate needs often dictate changing priorities for the project and the people involved. This can involve you in a continual process of reviewing your plans to modify work assignments, priorities and even occasionally the project objectives. In these circumstances you are highly dependent on effective communication at all levels to ensure you stay in control of the project. Control implies effective monitoring, tracking the progress and good action planning to deal promptly with problems when they occur. All these elements are the core of the **project control system** which you must establish before you can initiate the execution of any work. Starting the project work without the procedures essential to effective control will lead to your spending much more time than you would like in chasing information and finding out what is really happening.

Most organisations have established, even traditional, methods of monitoring and reporting progress of normal day to day operations. Often these are based on the premise that everything is going well unless someone shouts: "Help." This promotes an accepted practice that reports are historical evidence for the record and are only given scant attention unless something has gone wrong at some point. The time delay in such circumstances is not normally serious to organisational working. You must ensure that this apparent 'laissez-faire' approach is not allowed to develop for your project. Rapid response to problems and rapid information flow is essential to effective project control.

It is appropriate for you to review existing procedures and decide if they are applicable to your project. Unless the organisation is familiar with project work, the procedures you derive must be seen to have the support of senior management and the key stakeholders. In practice this means they must demonstrate ownership and conform to the same procedures! Do not get trapped into accepting an existing paper chase or try and derive a new one! Project control does require some essential paperwork, but this must be kept to a minimum and much of it can be standardised with simple formats. A further advantage is the time saved by everyone in the administration aspects of their work by using a consistent methodology.

When the procedures for effective project control are derived ensure you get these accepted and signed off by the stakeholders before the execution of work commences.

Organising the project

Project work demands a high level of inter-personal skill from you to effectively manage other people. This is even more true when some of those individuals who are required to make a contribution to your project do not report directly to you. Can you rely on on your ability to negotiate with other line managers and their staff to get agreement on actions and priorities for the work to be executed? Further, can you be sure the work will be carried out to the standards you require and even that the work content is clearly understood?

Normal day to day operations involve a high proportion of repetitive work that is clearly understood (most of the time) by those doing the work. Instructions can readily be given with minimal detail in the knowledge that they are understood because you assume the individual knows what is expected of him or her and can do the work to the required standards. When you allocate work in this way the expediency of time and the assumption of existing knowledge and skills apparently relieves you of the need to explain the detail and the consequences of late delivery of results or a lowering of quality. This state of affairs is not a criticism of how you work in normal operations, but it highlights the potential trap of complacency that can carry over into the work of the project. Can you be sure that instructions given and agreed verbally will be carried out on time?

You can assume that verbal instructions are sufficient but this approach is not consistent with the effort you have put into developing the plans. As a general rule your control is enhanced and made easier if the work is clearly documented and understood. This will minimise the risks of unnecessary work being executed and maintain focus on the important elements of the work content. Clear documentation also ensures that any individual's work is set in the right context of the whole project and the consequential effects of poor performance in any way is readily highlighted. A further benefit is the ease with which any individual working on the project can readily report progress in a definitive manner against a clear plan.

Of course you are now concluding that by the time you have documented the work of the project, it could have been executed and the team moved on to another project! In practice you do not need to document all the work at the outset – in fact you usually cannot. You only need to document the work a specific period ahead, a period that depends on the project size and duration. This could be two weeks, four weeks or even more, but it is pointless to go into the detail too far ahead as unforeseen changes to your plans may be necessary as the work proceeds.

At the same time that you derive the essential components of your project control system, you need to decide what minimal documentation is necessary to set out the work to be executed in each **key stage**. As the project progresses you continue to layer the plan **by developing the detail of each stage of the work breakdown structure** and setting this out on standard forms. This process ensures there is no doubt what has to be done and by whom and by when within the overall plan. Thus the planning process never really finishes until the project achieves the desired objectives.

The process of organising the project and establishing the control system requires you to establish clearly defined procedures that are acceptable to existing or future quality standards. This is particularly essential if the organisation has achieved certification to BS 5750 or is striving to achieve this standard in the near future.

The sections that follow examine how you can improve you project management in these two essential aspects of preparing to implement the project execution.

Summary

- Ensure all planning documents to date are signed off
- Review existing procedures for control
- Prepare to organise the project
- Continue to develop the Work Breakdown Structure to lower levels

2

Organising the Project

You can start to organise the project from the base point of the documents listed in Chapter 1. These documents constitute the **project plan baseline** upon which you now build the mechanical structure of the whole project, identifying all the individual tasks that are to be completed and by whom within the baseline time frames.

You need three essential working documents before you to start the process:

- The **Bar chart** or **Gantt chart**
- The Work Breakdown Structure
- The **Linear Responsibility Chart**

All of these now exist for the project **key stages** as a result of your earlier planning activities. However before you can start to organise the project any further you must re-examine the charts you have derived. For convenience here the term '**plan chart**' is used to indicate both the **bar chart** and the **Gantt chart** as you will be using only one of these forms of display, depending on whether you have used critical path analysis or not.

The plan chart is derived initially on the basis that each key stage or activity is carried out by one individual, working full-time for normal working hours. If you have not yet made any adjustments to the estimated durations for the real time estimates then now is the time to do so. There are probably few of the key stages that can be executed on a continuous full-time basis; most of the people who are assigned to carry out the project work are obliged to carry out other operational activities. The **linear responsibility chart** is your record of who has accepted responsibility for each of the key stages in the plan. This responsibility indicates the particular individual you have charged with ensuring that the actual work is carried out to the standards and quality you require. It does not necessarily mean that that individual does the work, particularly where it is carried out by other departments in the organisation. The responsible person must co-ordinate the work of others and report the status and progress to you as the project leader. It is therefore essential that those individuals to whom you have allocated responsibilities are aware of their obligations to you and the project. These people are the key members of your team, upon whom you must rely to remain committed to the work of the project.

Putting Real Time into the project

Before the project work can be implemented, you must review the **linear responsibility chart** you prepared earlier for the key stages and complete the information included in the chart. At this stage, if necessary, you can expose the plans to the functional managers as a group of stakeholders as you must negotiate the amount of resource time available to you. An example of a completed chart is shown in Figure 2.1.

Note the column headed 'TC'. This is your record of the amount of time contingency you have allowed in your planning for each of the key stages. This additional amount of time (in consistent units) is **included** in the total time for a key stage. You can keep the record separately if you do not want such data exposed, but do keep a record somewhere since the amount is not a constant factor. Alternatively record the data in your **Project Diary**. The latter is preferable if you need to record some reminder notes with the information. You must prepare yourself to pay particular attention to the critical activities in the plan, recording contingencies and alternative actions to take if progress appears to be hindered at any time.

The total project time you have derived must now be adjusted to show the effects of resource assignments for each key stage. At this point you may not have enough detailed information to complete all the resource assignments. In practice you only plan the detail a few key stages ahead so you must rely on discussion and agreement of the time required to complete the work of each key stage. This leads you to make 'contracts' with the individuals named in the **linear responsibility chart**. These contracts are critical

LINEAR RESPONSIBILITY CHART   SHEET *1* OF *1*

PROJECT: *PROJECT SCOR*   DRAWN BY: *TRD*   APPROVED BY: *JGW*

Project Leader: Terry Downs

Line No	KEY STAGE No: ALL CODE	DESCRIPTION	Durn. day wk mth	TC	RESPONSIBILIY NAME	J Williams	Terry Downs	Frank Harkness	Tony Bolton			
1	A	Locate Building	5	1	Terry Downs	D						
2	B	Plan layout	1	-	Frank Harkness		D,I					
3	C	Clean-up building	2	0.5	Joan Walton		I	M				
4	D	Get all approvals	4	1	Frank Harkness		I	M				
5	F	Quotes for mods	3	1	Frank Harkness	D	I	M				
6	L	Design fittings	4	1	Tony Bolton		I	D	M			
7	M	Install mods	5	0.5	Tony Bolton			I	M			
8	K	Design IT&C equipt.	6	1	Angela Hall	I	I	M				
9	G	Furniture quotes	8	2	Terry Downs	I	M					
10	N	Install fittings	3	0.4	Brian Golding			I	M			
11	P	Install IT&C equipt	2	0.2	Angela Hall		I	M				
12	R	Install office equipt	1	-	Tony Bolton		I		M			
13	H	Recruit staff	12	3	Joan Walton/Terry Downs	D	M					
14	S	Install furniture	1	-	Brian Golding		I		M			
15	T	Test IT&C equipt	2	0.4	Angela Hall	I	M					
16	U	Move staff	1	-	Frank Harkness		I	M				
17	E	Organise opening	1	-	Terry Downs	I	M					
18	V	Final testing	0.8	-	Angela Hall/Joan Walton	I	M					
19	W	Grand opening	0.2	-	Terry Downs	I	M					
20		Progress meetings			Terry Downs	I	M					
21												
22												

NOTES:
All times in weeks

Project Start Date; 19-6

Project Finish Date: 16-1

KEY:
M - Manages progress
C - Must be consulted
I - Must be informed
A - Available for advice
D - Decision taker

Date Issued: 21-5

Fig. 2.1   Linear Responsibility Chart for project SCOR

now to the execution phase of the project. The actual task list for each key stage is best derived in the **work breakdown structure**. Using this document you can quickly identify any group of tasks to be executed by each person in your team. Clearly you want to know from each individual how much time he or she has available to carry out the work he or she is obliged to complete. Additionally you need to be assured that the commitment agreed is realistic and achievable along with normal day to day operational duties that have to be completed. The capacity factor for each individual (the percentage of his or her total available time to carry out project work) is normally measured on a weekly basis, but any unit is acceptable as long as you use a consistent approach.

This process of deriving commitments for time is re-iterative and it may take you several discussions to arrive at acceptable results. Clearly a key stage that you have estimated to take five 'single-person days' to complete could only be completed in that time if there is adequate resource available i.e.

- one person full-time
- two people at 50% capacity
- three people at 33.3% capacity

Alternatively you may seek to complete the work early by increasing the resources if they are available and reduce the duration. If you are faced with the problem of reducing the total project time then this is clearly one of your options to examine in depth. This process of deriving commitments is reiterative and it may take some time to arrive at acceptable results – commitments that fit your plan requirements and are endorsed by the individual's manager.

Working with departmental representatives

The whole process is carried out with the individuals listed in the **linear responsibility chart** even though some of the actual work may be assigned to their colleagues or subordinates. This is particularly true where the work is done in other functional departments of the organisation. You can then adopt an alternative approach. Have a meeting with the responsible individual and agree in outline the work to be done and the timescale required to meet the current **plan chart** schedule. You must request that person to go away and derive a plan of the tasks to be carried out, the time each will take and who will be assigned the work. As the project leader you do not necessarily need to know who is doing the actual work, only that something is happening at the right time. Explain that each person executing a part of the work must give a forecast of how long it will take to complete.

As described before it is then essential to determine and agree the capacity factor – the proportion of time each has available to do the work. Collecting feedback of this data ensures that the responsible individual is not accepting the work without establishing that it can be completed on time. This helps to create a sense of ownership rather than your imposing the detail on others who do not directly report to you. The process ensures that anyone committed to work on your project is aware of his or her responsibilities and you get to know who is doing the different parts of the work.

Whether you are working directly with team members who do the work or collecting data from departmental representatives, you have one major problem to consider. How accurate are the individual estimates to carry out each task? Have realistic assessments been made of the possible interference factors to the work – reactive operational problems, unforeseen events, sickness and other absences from work and other interruptions? Like many project leaders before you, experience will soon give you a feeling of confidence in such data presented to you. You will develop your own 'rules of thumb' for people's forecasts (and those of different departments too) and apply your own factor to the suggested figures for security. Many organisations have established standards for **effective time** in the full working week to take account of these possible interference factors. Depending on the type of project work, the current loading level and the individual, this effective time can range from 3.0 to 4.5 days of a 'normal' five day week. For the sake of security decide by how much you will increase people's forecasts before accepting them in the final plan. This is particularly important when you are not in a position to approve or insist on overtime working to complete work.

The work plan

There are clearly some advantages in initiating a consistent format for deriving these detailed working plans. The people doing the work need to have clear instructions about what is expected of them, but you have to ensure that they are viewing the work plans in the same way as yourself. It is possible to prepare such a standard format to suit your needs and ask all departmental representatives to use this for feedback of planning information back to you. The same format is used for all detailed planning and for reporting progress at pre-determined regular intervals.

An example of a standardised **work plan sheet** for one of the key stages of an example, Project SCOR, is shown in Figure 2.2.

A benefit of this way of working is that you can be more confident that the work at the lower levels of the plan can be done on time. The planning has been subject to some detailed examination by the people who are doing the work. If the feedback to you is acceptable you can proceed in the knowledge that key stage is planned correctly. If the feedback indicates problems exist, you can get more closely involved to examine how to resolve the difficulties. The majority of difficulties encountered at this stage involve the availability of resources due to the normal operational activities of the individual or department. If the feedback indicates the time allocated to that key stage is unrealistic, then you will have to consider what action to take.

The options open to you are limited:

- seek additional resources
- use some of your contingency
- use up some of the **float time** (if non-critical)
- reduce the scope of the work
- review your objectives

Of course the last two on the list are normally not acceptable at this point in the project and will involve stakeholder consultation and approval. This limits your possible options for action even further. One other possible action may enter the equation. You can consider reducing some of the standards for the work to reduce time or allow less skilled people to do the work. This can lead to unfortunate results that eventually take more time because of the corrective action needed.

WORK PLAN RECORD

Key Stage No:	M - INSTALL MODIFICATIONS	Sponsor:	J. WILLIAMS
Work Plan Code:	WP/M/01	Project Leader:	TERRY DOWNS
		PROJECT:	SCOR
Scheduled Start Date:	12-9	Issued To:	TONY BOLTON	Account No:	SP/0734/592
Scheduled Finish Date:	17-10	Department:	OFFICE SERVICES	Budget Centre:	G0734-87
Scheduled Duration:	30 Days/Weeks/Months	CRITICAL ☒ NON-CRITICAL ☐	Sheet No.: 1 of 1

Code	ACTIVITIES	COMMENTS	Line No.
01	Deliver Materials	SUB-CONTRACT - B & H	1
02	Erect Office Partitions	B. H	2
03	Erect Meeting Rooms Partitions	B & H	3
04	Construct Board Room	B & H	4
05	Electrics & Special lighting	D.S Thompson & Son	5
06	ITAC Trunking installation	" —	6
07	Construct kitchenette	B & H	7
08	Plumbing extensions	John Fowles Services	8
09	Electrics in Kitchenette	D.S. Thompson & Son	9
10	Painting & Decorating	Harper & Co. Ltd	10
11	Carpet tiles throughout	Dewar Contract Flooring	11
			12

KEY STAGE SCHEDULE
Units: 2 □ per column
Days/Weeks/Months
0   10   20   30

ISSUE DATE:	2-9	Inform progress:	FRANK HARKNESS
		Available for advice:	FRANK HARKNESS
		Consult for problems:	TERRY DOWNS

Schedule agreed: T.Booth .... Operator
Schedule approved: Terry Downs .... Project Leader

Fig. 2.2 Work Plan Record

Eventually you arrive at acceptable solutions for the key stages undergoing detailed planning and enter the results into your plan chart.

Updating the plan

You now have sufficient data to update the information contained in the **plan chart** and the results may alter the whole appearance of the plan chart. As soon as the project work actually starts you monitor the commitments regularly. Changes in each individual's capacity factors can seriously affect your plan and you need to ensure that you are kept promptly informed through your reporting procedures of any changes that could cause you delays.

The process of deriving the work plans for each **key stage** is a continuous activity. As the project proceeds you anticipate forward by preparing the work plans for future key stages and reviewing any changes to the overall plan that may be necessary. Where changes occur it is obviously important that these are communicated clearly to the team and the stakeholders and you get acceptance and approval by the latter.

When you are satisfied you have planned the detail sufficiently to implement the project work you can prepare the **plan chart** for issue and 'freeze' this as the **baseline plan**. If your initial estimating is accurate and this is confirmed by the work plans for the first few key stages, the **plan chart** will not need any further updating before issuing to the stakeholders. The baseline includes all the supporting documents to describe the plan and how it is executed. It is 'frozen' to avoid confusion in everyone's mind about what was originally agreed. Any changes that take place from this point in time are recorded with reasons for the change, but the original is not destroyed. As you track progress you compare the actual performance against the baseline since this gives everyone involved valuable learning points for the future. Figure 2.3 shows part of the **plan chart** for Project SCOR before and after updating from the initial key stage **work plans**.

Whenever any changes are made to a **plan chart**, remember to record the revision with number, date and a keyword or two to indicate why the change is being made. In the example of Figure 2.3 the planned finish date has not changed but the scheduled completion dates for critical key stages have been amended.

The preparation of separate **work plans** for each of the **key stages** is an activity that requires you to impose some discipline upon the project process. Planning detail at the lower levels is an essential process to which many project leaders give scant attention. It is relatively easy to make assumptions about people's ability and their understanding of what is required for the project. Mistakes are expensive in terms of both finance and time and the causes are frequently inadequate communications. Inevitably failure to plan effectively at these levels will lead to problems, putting you in a continuous **reactive mode**. Using the procedures proposed here puts you into a continuous **pro-active mode** allowing you more time to react to problems when they occur.

In the examples given, the planning of detail is confined to just two levels by expanding each **key stage** into its component task list. As the project gets larger and more detailed you may find it necessary to go to a third or

PROJECT PLANNING CHART

PROJECT: _PROJECT SCOR_   KEY STAGE No: _ALL_

SHEET _1_ OF _1_   DRAWN BY: _TRD_   APPROVED BY: _GBW_

Line No	CODE	DESCRIPTION	Dun. day/wk/mth	RESOURCE NAME
1	A	Locate Building	5	Terry Downs
2	B	Plan layout	1	Frank Harkness
3	C	Clean-up building	1	Joan Watson
4	D	Get all approvals	5	Frank Harkness
5	F	Quotes for mods	5	Frank Harkness
6	L	Design fittings	3	Tony Bolton
7	M	Install mods	5	Tony Bolton
8	K	Design IT&C equipt.	5	Angela Hall
9	G	Furniture quotes	8	Terry Downs

CRITICAL PATH LINE

PROJECT PLANNING CHART

PROJECT: _PROJECT SCOR_   KEY STAGE No: _ALL_

SHEET _1_ OF _1_   DRAWN BY: _TRD_   APPROVED BY: _GBW_

Line No	CODE	DESCRIPTION	Dun. day/wk/mth	RESOURCE NAME
1	A	Locate Building	5	Terry Downs
2	B	Plan layout	1	Frank Harkness
3	C	Clean-up building	2	Joan Watson
4	D	Get all approvals	4	Frank Harkness
5	F	Quotes for mods	3	Frank Harkness
6	L	Design fittings	4	Tony Bolton
7	M	Install mods	5	Tony Bolton
8	K	Design IT&C equipt.	6	Angela Hall
9	G	Furniture quotes	8	Terry Downs

CRITICAL PATH LINE

Fig. 2.3   Project Chart – Real Time Updating

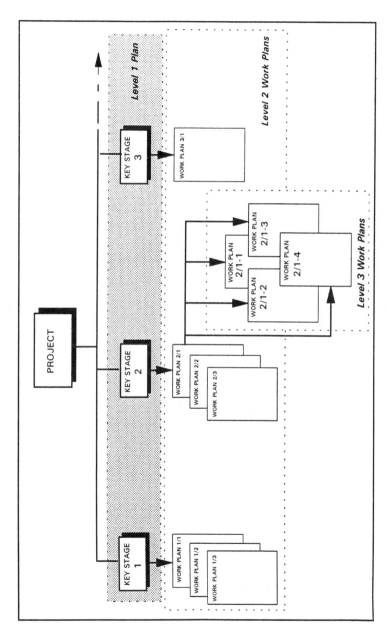

Fig. 2.4   Development of a Family of Work Plans

fourth level with some of the tasks within a **key stage**. The preparation of **work plans** is still essential at every level for the reasons given earlier. The larger project then has a complete family of **work plans** related to each parent **key stage** as shown in Figure 2.4. This is based on your initial derivation of the **work breakdown structure** making it easy to see where further detailed planning is needed before the work starts. The same documentation is also the basis for your derivation of financial information for the preparation of budget sheets for each key stage.

Now that you have completed the planning of the initial key stages and derived a final schedule that you feel meets the expectations of the stakeholders you can effectively launch your project.

Summary

- Review and update the Linear Responsibility Chart
- Identify capacity factors for each individual
- Put real time into the plans
- Where appropriate appoint Departmental Representatives
- Derive the Work Plans for the initial Key Stages
- Update the plan charts
- Continue to develop a family of work plans

3

The Control System

The control of the project process is a management function carried out by the project leader to ensure that the plans are executed as originally intended or subsequently modified to meet the project objectives. There is no mystique about controlling a project since it requires you to employ the same skills as managing any team of people with clear objectives. The difficulties usually arise because many project leaders are appointed to lead a project having had little or no experience of leading a team. In addition as the project leader you are frequently faced with the need to get things done by people enjoying a higher status than yourself in the organisational hierarchy. These difficulties enhance the need to establish some ground rules for your project to ensure that you maintain control at all times.

In organisations that are familiar with the project process and have established a project methodology from past experience, a set of procedures for control may already exist. These may not necessarily be fully appropriate for your project and you must review these and assess if they can provide the raw information you need. If no procedures exist then now is the time to set about deriving some with your team.

Controlling the project is a three step process:

- measuring progress towards an objective
- evaluating what remains to be done
- deriving action plans to achieve the right results

The **control system** is the methodology you employ through clearly defined procedures to ensure that the project stays on track towards the objectives desired by the stakeholders. The whole purpose of the system is to allow you to effectively:

- collect information about what is really happening
- compare this with what you have planned to happen
- analyse the variances exposed
- derive actions you can reasonably take
- implement action plans to keep the project on track

The process inevitably brings you and your team into contact with other departments, managers and their staff and you need to have an understanding of their working methods and priorities combined with strong interpersonal skills. Essential to enable you to carry out the activities for control are your **job description** and **statement of authority** established at the conceptual phase when the project was initiated.

The control system is therefore concerned to identify **variances** as shown in Figure 3.1 with regular monitoring, feedback, analysis and action planning. This is not an

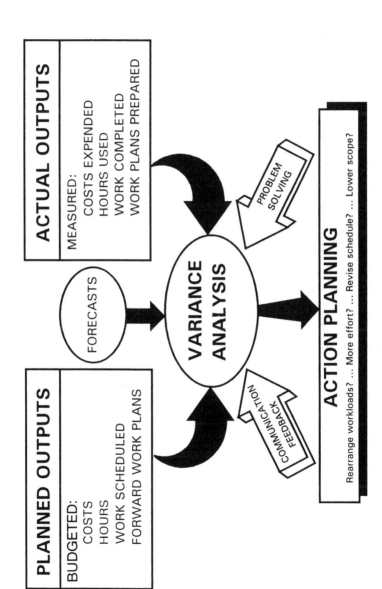

Fig. 3.1   The Project Control System

activity you can assign or delegate in entirety. You are accountable to your key stakeholders for the performance of all aspects of the project process and must make and take decisions, however difficult or painful out of concern for **the project**. However much you trust the members of your team there are always some decisions that remain yours if you are to maintain control and justify these to your sponsor.

The control of the project also brings into sharp focus the need to use all your skills of managing people to develop and maintain teamwork. You must overcome many barriers that occur owing to the differences between project management and functional management. You cannot maintain a parochial view of the work to be done. As Figure 3.1 shows, the analysis for variance between the planned and actual outputs has several inputs. Apart from your direct observation and measurement through normal monitoring processes, good communication is an essential element of ensuring that the right things are being measured by others to standards you have established. This requires you to explain how and why you are collecting data and taking honest and constructive feedback on the methods used. If these are not working effectively then you must act promptly to ensure that the correct information is collected. The same comments apply to analysis of the raw data and it is obviously important for a consistent approach and method to be used by everyone.

One of the difficulties often experienced in project work is the actual measurement of the amount of work completed by an individual or department. This is subjective based on the level of detail you agreed when the work plans were originally derived and issued. In practice the use of **percentage completion** is a convenient measurement to feed into your tracking process. It is easy to mark this measurement into the bars of a Gantt Chart or Bar Chart to demonstrate the amount of work done up to any point in time. Unfortunately most errors in project work derive from over- optimistic estimating of the time to complete a particular piece of work. The result is a potential source of misunderstanding. The graphic display of the project plan has a significant shortcoming here. You cannot easily show the variation of the 'work rate' in an activity duration bar, since it is assumed to be essentially linear with time. The peaks and troughs in the rate at which work should be completed is not shown and some parts are carried out faster than others. The rate also varies with different individuals.

One way to overcome this shortcoming is to ask individual team members separately to give you a forecast of how long it will take to complete a piece of work, based on the time taken to date with their current output rate. This allows the individual to assess output in his or her current situation with other work and priorities, compared to estimates made, maybe, several weeks earlier. This also gives you better control of the situation and the opportunity to take any relevant decisions about getting more effort on the work.

Even with the best and most detailed plans, problems occur and you must take the necessary steps to identify the causes and derive solutions promptly. Using the appropriate problem solving techniques provides rapid inputs to using the analysis of variances and deriving the most likely actions to give acceptable results and bring the project back on track.

Essential reporting procedures

Control of the project process is therefore dependent on your establishing some clearly defined procedures that must be used without exception by everyone involved. You have established some firm procedures for the derivation of the project plans so you now extend these into the control system. It is a good practice to involve the team in this work and sometimes it is valid to consult the key stakeholders, particularly since the plans and procedures must finally be signed off as approved before launching the project.

Your work plans include an opportunity for you to identify the people involved in each part of the project so you must establish how you are to get regular feedback of the progress of the work. You must decide if you can rely on personal monitoring or verbal reports, particularly if there are several other departments involved. As a minimum two aspects of the work are required:

- progress of the work plans issued
- deviations from scheduled activities

Why written reports?

If the work is all confined to your own department it is tempting to rely on verbal inputs on the grounds that the people are probably located near you. However you still have to record the progress and this then loads you with an additional administrative activity.

Verbal reporting makes people lazy and lacking in discipline in the reporting activity. Demanding concise written reports reinforces your attempts to encourage order and discipline in the team with good work practices. People are more likely to be honest about reporting progress in writing when they have to sign the form. The ambush meeting on the corridor or in the car park is hardly conducive to getting accurate feedback of progress, but is more likely to tell you what you want to hear – so they can make a quick getaway!

It is also unlikely that you can avoid some inputs from other functional areas, so reporting is better considered as a formal process, using a standard format **progress report** for all involved. Design a simple form that gives you just the raw data you need, avoiding demands for large amounts of information. If you find you require more at any point you can follow up with a face to face meeting with the team member to discuss the work. A suggested format is given in Figure 3.2 that is readily modified to suit your needs.

The frequency of reporting is established either as a project norm or varied at your discretion according to the type of work, the individual person and the department. As a norm weekly reports must be an obvious choice, but less frequent reports are justifiable in longer term projects.

When weekly reports are employed it is not necessary to call for monthly written reports that just summarise what you have previously received. You can keep the rest of the team informed of progress through regular team meetings or, if necessary, distribution (selectively) of weekly reports.

Recording deviations

An important aspect of control is prompt identification of deviations from the plan. Although your monitoring and feedback through reports when analysed can allow you to derive conclusions about progress, there is always

Key Stage No:		PROGRESS REPORT			
Work Plan Code:		PROJECT:			
Scheduled Date:					
Sponsor:		Account No:			
Project Leader:		Budget Centre:			
Report By:		Circulation:			
Department:					

TASK ID CODE	SCHEDULED DURATION	DESCRIPTION	COMPLETION DATE		SLIPPAGE
			SCHEDULED	FORECAST	

Comments:

Prepared By:	Checked By:	Approved By:
Date:	Date:	Date:

Fig. 3.2   Format for Progress Reports

the possibility that corrective action is too late and only damage limitation remains. Occasions can arise where deviations that lead to variances can be identified early or even anticipated. In such situations an early warning system is valuable using an **Exception Report** that is also a standard format. An example is shown in Figure 3.3.

You must ensure that everyone involved with the project is aware of the need to use the Exception Report promptly if a deviation is anticipated or discovered. These deviations can apply to hours, costs, work done or any other criteria you decide. The essential requirement is that you are informed as a matter of immediate urgency if a deviation occurs, especially one that cannot be resolved by the individual concerned. The Exception Report can also be used to communicate to you and others in good time if anything unusual or unexpected occurs that may seriously affect the progress of the project in any way.

The Exception Report must be given a high priority status by everyone in the project team and you need to continually emphasise that it is in everyone's interest to report promptly on these forms when appropriate. This is where your team building efforts will show a payback because an effective team always shows concern for disciplined process and effective communication.

It may also be valid to keep a complete 'at a glance' record or log of all Exception Reports issued during the project. You can easily do this by using a summary record form as shown in Figure 3.4.

Any failure to use these process elements of the team's activities through not complying with agreed procedures must be regarded as a serious deficiency of teamworking.

Key Stage No:	**EXCEPTION REPORT**	
Work Plan Code:		
Scheduled Date:	**PROJECT:**	
Sponsor:	Account No:	
Project Leader:	Budget Centre:	
Report By:	Circulation:	
Department:		

Details of deviation from schedule:

Reasons for the deviation:

Consequencies of the noted deviation:

Forecast completion date:

Financial implications:

	Scheduled Budget:
	Actual cost to date:
	Forecast overspend:

Comments:

Prepared By:	Checked By:	Approved By:
Date:	Date:	Date:

Fig. 3.3   Format for Exception Reports

Project:			SUMMARY LOG - EXCEPTION REPORTS	
REPORT NO:	DATE ISSUED	ISSUED BY:	DEVIATION REPORTED	ACTION TAKEN BY:
Comments:				
Prepared By: Date:		Checked By: Date:		Approved By: Date:

Fig. 3.4   Format for Summary Log Record – Exception Reports

This is an aspect of monitoring that must have your close attention at all times. Individual effort can easily be wasted through poor communication and failure to maintain progress awareness in the team, particularly where deviations from the plan have occurred that have serious consequential effects on certain parts of the work.

Changes to the baseline plan

Few projects enjoy the luxury of being implemented and completed without some changes to the baseline plan. You believe you and your team have put considerable effort into planning the **key stage plan** and then developed the detail of these stages as the project progresses. However you should presume some changes are going to occur and prepare everyone to take a flexible approach to accepting the need to accommodate changes that are clearly essential to achieving the project objectives. This is not to suggest that you must accept all changes, because some are bound to need debate before acceptance or rejection. Some of the reasons why they occur include:

- Over-optimistic estimating of time for the work
- Omission of one or more stages/activities/tasks
- Lack of available resource(s) at the critical time when needed
- Loss of resource(s) part way through some critical work
- Strategic change of priorities during project implementation
- Loss of senior management interest and support
- Change of financial emphasis/availability of funding
- Stakeholder 'change of mind' about objectives
- Process 'overload' – interference due to increase of other workload

- Process system failure – authorisations/decisions not made on time
- Poor teamwork and co-ordination

The control system is designed to sound the warning signals if any of these potential 'change leaders' occur through the measurement of what is actually happening during implementation and execution of the work. Any significant change leads to the project, or part of it, going into a hold position until you can assess the implications.

The implications of any change are profound both on the people involved and the project itself. Your primary concern is always for your project and then you can attempt to deal with the people problems resulting from the change and the action plans you derive. Changes of any sort, regardless of size, must be recorded and approved before implementation. Certain changes are approved by you within your own limits of authority, to enable the project to progress. Others may require acceptance and approval by one or more stakeholders. It is essential you do not rely on verbal acceptance, but use some standard form for recording the change, its implications and the acceptance and approval 'sign-off' principle.

A typical standard format for this recording and approval process is shown in Figure 3.5. Again for larger projects it is useful to maintain a summary of all changes recorded during the implementation and execution of the project as shown in Figure 3.6. The use of these forms is essential to effective project control, promoting communication to those involved and keeping them informed of what is actually happening. Along with the other report forms described they are the key documentation to come out of monitoring and tracking of your project. (see Chapter 5)

Key Stage No:	**CHANGE REQUEST**
Work Plan Code:	
Scheduled Date:	**PROJECT:**
Sponsor:	Account No:
Project Leader:	Budget Centre:
Report By:	Circulation:
Department:	

Details of proposed change from current plan/schedule:

Do stakeholders need to be informed: YES   NO   By whom: When:

Reasons for the change:

Consequencies of the proposed change:

Revised Forecast completion date if change approved:

Financial implications:

	Scheduled Budget:
	Actual cost to date:
	Cost of change:

Comments:	**IMPLEMENT BY:**
	DEFER UNTIL:
Decision required by:	**REJECTED:**

Prepared By:	Checked By:	Approved By:
Date:	Date:	Date:

Fig. 3.5   Format for Change Request Report

Project:	SUMMARY LOG - CHANGE REQUESTS				
REPORT NO:	DATE ISSUED	ISSUED BY:	CHANGE REQUESTED	APPROVED BY:	ACTION TAKEN BY:
Comments:					
Prepared By: Date:		Checked By: Date:		Approved By: Date:	

Fig. 3.6   Format for Summary Log Record – Change Requests

Project progress meetings

It would be unthinkable to consider executing a project without progress meetings – or would it really? You must ask yourself what you want from having regular progress meetings. It is easy to regard such meetings as essential because all managers have them in every department. In practice managers know team meetings are essential to team building and effective teamworking. Both are essential in project work but how many meetings do you attend where teamwork is never discussed or even mentioned? Meetings generally happen because tradition dictates they must take place, not necessarily because they are an essential part of team process. Many hours of productive time get wasted in meetings so it is important to establish why you have progress meetings and what they are to achieve.

If a meeting is defined as **a recorded, structured communication activity between two or more people with a specific purpose** to distinguish it from just conversation or day to day technical discussion, then four types of meeting are used in project work:

- informal regular 1:1 meetings with team members
- informal short team meetings
- formal project progress meetings
- formal project review meetings (involving key stakeholders)

Each has a place in your control system, depending on the size and duration of the project. It is important that you identify the needs of the project for any of these meetings and then set up a clear schedule before implementation of the work. All the essential meetings must be diarised by the attendees well in advance so that there is no excuse for not attending. Each type of meeting has a specific purpose and you must establish the ground rules for them at the outset. Conducting meetings is a further leadership skill you must develop if they are to achieve their purpose. This is discussed further in Chapter 6.

Summary

- Decide how you can measure progress
- Derive Reporting procedures to adopt
- Establish Deviation and Exception Report formats
- Ensure that everyone understands what is expected of them
- Establish format and procedures for Change Requests
- Get the control system and documentation signed off

4

Launching the Project

Now that you have organised your **control system** and established the formats for the minimum reports you expect to receive you are prepared to implement the execution phase of the project.

Although the team members have been allocated responsibilities within the project it is equally important that where they do not normally report directly to you, their functional manager is clearly aware of these obligations. Up to now you have had direct discussions and negotiation with these managers to secure the release of their staff to work on the project. If the functional manager of any team member is not made aware of the responsibilities you are giving that person, then you risk potential problems of prioritising workloads in the future. It is obviously better if you have entered into some form of 'contract' with other managers before the work starts. This avoids or minimises the risk of conflict later during project execution, when delays due to time expended on resolving conflict situations can be serious.

Of course the discussions you have had with these other managers in the organisation have been limited in scope while you are planning the project. Your planning work to date has, of necessity, involved individuals from other departments and their managers must know what has been happening. Now you are expecting the workload for some of these people to increase as the project work starts. So if you have not had any detailed discussion with other functional managers, then now is the time to initiate that activity. You need to get commitment from the team members **and** their functional managers if you are to achieve success. By now you will have done enough with your team members to build that commitment, through the work you have carried out together during the planning phase.

To build that commitment with the functional managers, call them together with the project team and key stake-holders for a short presentation of the project plans. Insist that your project sponsor attends and opens the presentation, stressing:

- the project context in corporate terms
- the priorities in strategic terms
- who the key players are – the project structure
- the project objectives
- the importance of their co-operation and ongoing support

You can only get the support and commitment of this group if they have belief in your ability to achieve success and you can demonstrate that the resources they are providing are planned to be used effectively. This is your opportunity to present your carefully constructed plans, explaining the details and resourcing schedules. You must convince the managers that you have total confidence in your plans and demonstrate your enthusiasm and commitment for the project. Explain that you intend to keep them informed of the project progress at regular intervals – remember, these people are your **stakeholders**. Ask them to help by keeping you informed of any changes in their departmental workloads that could, at any moment, affect the release of their staff from normal operational duties. Project work is always vulnerable to unforeseen reactive operational situations and you must be flexible to meet these challenges when they occur. If you have planned carefully and assessed the potential risks, you will have established contingency plans for the areas of support you see as the most vulnerable.

You can regard this meeting as the **Project Launch Meeting** where you seek to ensure that all those involved with the project in any way are brought together to understand their roles and the outcomes you are seeking to achieve. You are seeking their full support so at this meeting start as you intend to continue. Issue everyone with a brief information pack containing:

- A list of who is directly involved and their roles
- The Scope of Work statement
- The Objectives statement
- The Plan Chart – showing Level 1 details
- The Linear Responsibility Chart
- Copies of reporting formats

You can also suggest that you will attempt to keep them informed of progress through personal contact (if the work carried out in any of their department represents a large part of any key stage). Remember that they are busy people, just like you, so do keep the presentation as short as possible – say 30 minutes, then allow a short time for a question and answer session.

Use the opportunity to ensure that people have the chance to talk to one another and the 'getting to know each other' process will lead to better understanding in the team. Stakeholders' expectations will inevitably be discussed in such conversations and it is not unusual for some hidden agendas to be partially, but inadvertently, exposed! If possible arrange the meeting to finish at lunchtime with a buffet lunch for everyone. The informal climate will assist you to build teamwork and co-operation in the group.

Summary

- Set up a meeting of all stakeholders and the project team
- Prepare a presentation of the project plans
- Prepare summary plan documents to distribute
- Ask the sponsor to make an opening speech
- Hold the Launch Meeting

5

Monitoring and Tracking

After the initial euphoria of the Project Launch Meeting your first concern must be to generate and maintain the momentum of the project work. The finalised plans have been 'frozen' as the **baseline plan** and you are now concerned to ensure the work is done on time and to the standards you have established for the project. You have identified the project **success factors** and how these are to be measured but it is still worth checking that everyone involved is clear about how you will determine the progress.

Monitoring is the process of checking that everything is going well and according to the plan. You cannot assume that if you hear nothing from team members, then all is well! It probably means that you have forgotten something and everyone is waiting for you to make some decisions. You can only monitor effectively through personal contact with each team member who is carrying out project work. You need to verify that:

- The work is progressing according to the plan schedules
- There has been no change of priorities for the individual
- There are no problems being encountered
- There are no problems anticipated
- Nothing has been forgotten in the planning stage
- Project costs are running within budget

In addition you must have regular contact with the **key stakeholders** to maintain their support and commitment to the project. This is particularly important if the organisation does not have a Project Steering Committee. Then you must rely on contact with the project sponsor to keep you informed of any changes to corporate needs from the project or any change of strategic priorities with changing business conditions. Some stakeholders may have committed to execute some of the work of the project and you must monitor their performance in the same way as any other team member. The fact that some of these stakeholders have a higher status than yourself is irrelevant in terms of the the project; they must expect to have their performance monitored.

Tracking is the process of taking the results of monitoring and the outputs from the project **control system** to update the plan and compare the overall results with the baseline plan. You take the status and progress reports that you have verified and use this information to ensure that the right work is being done at the right time, in the right order and to the standards you set. The major problem associated with tracking is deciding how progress is measured. You need to update your **Plan Charts** to show graphically the status of the project at any particular point. This leads inevitably to the simple question: "What is the percentage completion on your work plan?" Unfortunately this can only lead to a response that gives you a subjective assessment of what has happened so far. Provided there have been no problems identified to you by the individual doing the work, you are really more concerned to know about what still has to be done. Your initial estimates of time to carry out a particular package of work has been derived from:

■ A time estimate agreed by discussion with the individual
■ An assessment of the individual's capacity for project work

Both are subject to potentially huge errors, even though you may have built in some contingency to the data you used in your baseline plan. This can compensate, to some extent, errors in estimating. But you can never accurately assess the capacity of an individual to execute the work. As indicated earlier you can use some 'rules of thumb' for estimating the capacity of any individual to take on project work. But many factors can cause the initial agreement to be useless:

■ The individual has found the work takes longer than expected
■ Lack of confidence
■ Change of priorities from the individual's manager
■ Lack of interest (and motivation)
■ Absence from work

Monitoring can help you to identify the presence of any of these factors affecting the progress of the work, but even then it is sometimes difficult to be absolutely sure what has caused progress to deviate from the plan schedule.

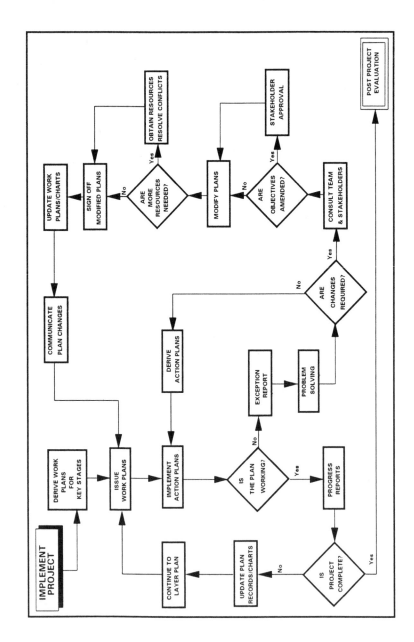

Fig. 5.1 The Monitoring and Tracking Process

When asking for the status of any work package, it is obviously more important to have an updated estimate of how much time the individual expects to need to complete the work. By asking for a **forecast to completion** you are proactively seeking a review of the factors that influence the individual's capacity to execute the work according to the schedules.

The process of monitoring and tracking is illustrated in the flow diagram shown in Figure 5.1. The process comprises three inter-dependent dynamic cycles:

■ The 'normal progress' cycle
■ The 'problem solving' cycle
■ The 'change' cycle

Each of these involve inter-dependent activities at different times, according to the status of your project and its progress towards achieving the desired objectives.

The 'Normal Progress' cycle

At the start of the implementation phase of your project you issue the agreed work plans for the initial key stages of the project. This is often a critical stage as you attempt to get the work moving at the right pace. Remember you are now asking people to actually start fulfilling their commitments and the additional workload they have agreed to accept. This requires you to be especially vigilant in monitoring to ensure there is no early slippage. The initial enthusiasm can readily be killed off by problems or changes of priority forced on people by their managers without informing you. Your effective monitoring will identify if there are any problems or whether the plan is working well.

If everything is going well, you receive status reports to the format you have set up as standard. As the project is not yet complete, you use this information to update the project records – specifically the Plan Chart and work plans. In the meantime you continue to layer the plan, deriving the work plans for subsequent key stages and agreeing the priorities with those individuals who are to execute the work. As the work progresses to schedule you can issue these new work plans at the appropriate time in accordance with the plan.

There is a potential trap here because you may be tempted to issue some work plans earlier than originally scheduled. Remember that you have clearly identified your logic and the inter-dependencies of the key stages. Issuing work plans early may lead people to believe they can start work earlier than scheduled with an apparent bonus of time available, particularly if they are under capacity at the time. However if data or results from an earlier key stage are needed to complete such work there is a risk involved. Rather than wait, some preliminary, unchecked data is used or assumptions are made on minimal information. The result is often a need for re-work later with potentially serious adverse time and cost consequences.

If your own monitoring or progress reports coming to you indicate problems are developing you must first verify if it is the plan at fault or the individual who is doing the work. Before issuing an **exception report** carry out some simple checks:

- Is the relevant work plan correct?
- Are the scheduled estimates accurate?
- Has something been forgotten,ignored or assumed?
- Have costs run away from budget?

- Has the individual insufficient skills?
- Is the individual overloaded with other work?

One or more of these questions may give you clues to identifying the potential problem before issuing a report. This action will lead you and your team into the next cycle – **'problem solving'**.

The 'Problem Solving' cycle

The issue of an **exception report** presumes that you are going to take some further action. Something has gone wrong although this may not directly result from your original plans. Quite possibly inadequacy in planning may show itself in this way, or you and your team are facing the unforeseen circumstances that you can always expect to happen at some point. In the interests of the project, your main concern now is to derive a solution to the problem identified, not dwell on why it has happened or who you can blame. You can return later to evaluating these aspects of the problem in order that everyone learns from the possible mistakes that have been made.

Problem solving is a re-iterative process requiring some discipline to arrive at the best possible solution. It is very easy to fall into the trap of using a 'gut reaction' to solve a problem quickly. Invariably this involves jumping in to draw conclusions from incomplete or biased information without developing alternative courses of action.

When a problem occurs in an activity that is regarded as routine and within an individual's capability, then negative feelings are experienced by the individual. The problem is a nuisance, seen as interfering with the work especially when it is perceived as having been caused by some external factor or person. This can lead to depression, frustration and demotivation and as a consequence the schedule starts to slip. Some people are observed to regard problems as a form of failure and they will use many devious means from avoidance to hiding the facts, in order to pretend that there is no problem really and that there is no perception of failure.

The reverse is really true since you must regard problems in a positive manner, even as opportunities for:

- deriving a better way of doing something (there always is one)
- learning from the experience
- developing teamworking

Of course you are not going to fall into the trap of treating just symptoms when a problem occurs. Symptoms are perceived effects and everyone involved has different perceptions and beliefs about why the problem ever occurred. Giving rapid response first-aid only affects the existing symptoms, not the root cause of the problem. Unfortunately the perceived symptoms can change and since you have not examined and dealt with the root cause, the new symptoms may be perceived as a new, unrelated problem. The first step to understanding a problem is to write down a clear statement of the problem as perceived and its consequential effects. This **problem statement** is the basis from which you and your team can develop an agreed solution. The process of problem solving follows a sequence of activities as shown in Figure 5.2.

Deriving solutions to problems is an ideal opportunity for you to reinforce your teamworking. Involving the team

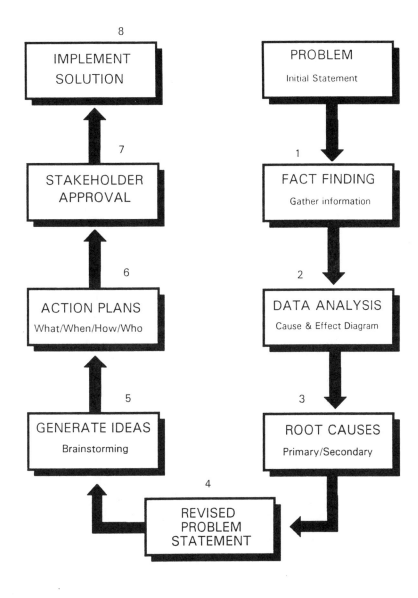

Fig. 5.2 The Problem Solving Process

in each step of the above process is likely to generate better solutions. More importantly, it creates ownership and commitment to implementing the action plans you derive to resolve the problem and get the project back on track as quickly as possible.

The techniques you can use for problem solving are described in more detail in Chapter 7. When you have followed the process through the stages to deriving some alternative solutions (or occasionally only one possible solution) you make the final decision. Before you can derive any **action plan** to implement correction to the exception report you must consider two questions:

- "Does the action required need stakeholder approval?"
- "Does the action required involve a significant change to the plan?"

Unless it is a minor matter it is usually prudent to get the action plan approved by the **key stakeholders**, since they will be aware of the problem anyway from the exception report you issued earlier. You can proceed to implement the action plan, briefing the team and any other people involved about exactly what each is expected to do to bring the project back on track.

Remember to record on the exception report the actions you take and who is given responsibility for ensuring they are implemented promptly. If there is a significant change to the plan then you must move into the change cycle in Figure 5.1.

The 'Change' cycle

Any problem that points to a significant change to the original plan must be examined in detail. Although you take a flexible approach there are clearly limits to how much change you can accommodate within the agreed budgets and timescales. Again you are faced with some important decisions that are based on answers you seek from some fundamental questions:

- "Does the change affect the key stage budget and timescale?"
- "Does the change affect the project budget and timescale?"
- "Does the change limit the achievement of the objectives?"
- "Does the change suggest the objectives should be modified?"
- "Does the change create a need for more resources?"
- "Does the change have an implication on other projects?"
- "Should the project go on 'hold' to carry out a full review?"
- "Should the project be aborted now?"

The answers to all these and possibly other questions help you in the process of decision taking for a subsequent course of action. Your first step is to consult the team to determine the consequential effects of the proposed change. You need to establish the financial implications and determine if the budget is adversely affected. If there are additional costs involved then these must be clearly derived and the variation to the project budget analysed. It is possible that an overspend in one key stage can be recovered through careful control of other key stages. Alternatively you may consider seeking authority to utilise some of the project contingency fund. Similarly the resource needs are re-assessed to determine if additional skills and people are required. You may consider you can achieve the results needed without extra resources by reviewing and re-assigning responsibilities on the **linear responsibility chart**.

At the same time you can form a judgement about the project timescale.

Changes within one key stage are possibly containable within the stage without subsequent damage to the rest of your schedule. This is where you can return to a detailed examination of available **float times** to explore how much the key stage activities can be moved, expanded or reduced to limit damage to the project schedule. Just loading additional resources into the project plan does not automatically correct many problems. In practice such action is more likely to create more problems for you than it actually solves! The **Gantt chart** is a very useful tool for you now, showing clearly the consequences of each alternative action you have as an option.

This 'what if' analysis can help you to make the right decision provided that you have spent time collecting all the known background data. The point of all this analysis is to avoid jumping to conclusions about the project objectives. Your careful attention to detail assists you to decide if the approved project objectives are still valid (including deadlines) or whether some change is required. If a change is obviously needed then you must propose the amendments to the key stakeholders and seek their early agreement and 'sign off'.

This step in the process is a potential threat to your project. Getting an approval and 'sign off' decision may take time. Just when you need them, key stakeholders seem to have a habit of being absent from their office or on holiday or procrastination rules! It's common to hear statements like: "We're considering your proposals, just leave it with me." Unfortunately that is just what happens, it gets left – and left – and left. Perhaps it is hoped the problem will disappear if nothing is done. This is a possibility, but a very slim one for project work. When putting forward your proposals for a change to the objectives you must indicate a reasonable timescale for the decision to be made. However you must also clearly set out the consequences of delay to the decision and you can do this by using the existing project documentation. In certain situations you may have to resort to taking authority and the decision yourself in the interests of keeping the project moving ahead. Do remember to record accurately what you decide and do inform the key stakeholders promptly.

This is not likely to happen if you have consulted the key stakeholders early in the change cycle and have received their input. They may even authorise you informally to proceed anyway and just inform them after action has been taken. Record the informal authorisation also!

Once the objectives are revised where appropriate and approved, you can proceed to finalise the plan amendments that you need to implement. You review your resource needs and check that there is no conflict existing for any individual involved:

- within the project workload – no obvious overload
- between the project workload and their operational activities

If there is a clear need to do more work in the same timescale you must decide what skills are needed and seek additional resources from elsewhere but within the project authorised financial constraints.

Finally you update the project documentation and put forward your modified plans for stakeholder 'sign off'. With that approval you prepare or update the affected **work plans**. If these exist and you are amending them, remember to record the revision date on the work plan form. You set up a team meeting to communicate to the team the agreed changes and the implementation of the action plans to keep the project moving.

With the issuing of the revised **work plans** you are back in the 'normal progress' cycle of monitoring. Of course the project has not been on hold while you are resolving problems or planning changes. Much of the work is ongoing and unaffected by problems and minor changes and you must continue to monitor and demonstrate your concern for the project progress. If a major change is highlighted or exposed as essential then you have to quickly consider whether you can justify putting the whole project on 'hold'. To do this effectively you must issue a **hold notification** to all the stakeholders and individuals involved.

This is a serious step and it creates potential difficulties for you later:

- People are demotivated
- Your leadership skills are questioned
- People get loaded with other work
- The teamwork suffers and fragments
- Takes time to get back on track

Your primary concern is to keep the project moving and maintain key stakeholder commitment through a high confidence level in your ability to deliver the project objectives. Through careful monitoring and tracking with the appropriate procedures you are sure to succeed.

Summary

Decide how you intend to monitor progress

- Decide responsibilities for tracking
- Establish the monitoring process and communicate it
- Explain what you expect from the team
- Explain how deviation and exception reports are to be used
- Ensure that the team members know about problem solving techniques
- Explain how Change Requests are to be used
- Ensure that team members understand all procedures

6

Meetings

A significant part of your own management time is taken up by meetings and since project work is about getting results, anything you can do to reduce 'talking' and increase 'doing' is a worthwhile activity. As the project leader you need different types of meetings through the project life cycle:

- Regular informal 1:1 sessions with team members
- Regular project team meetings
- Negotiation meetings with functional managers
- Project review meetings with key stakeholders

These represent the minimum, since you may also have meetings for negotiation with suppliers and external consultants. Each has a different purpose but with one overall objective – to support the project management process. So meetings are inevitable but that does not mean you become a slave to the activity and allow them to become a disorganised, unstructured, demotivating and time-wasting

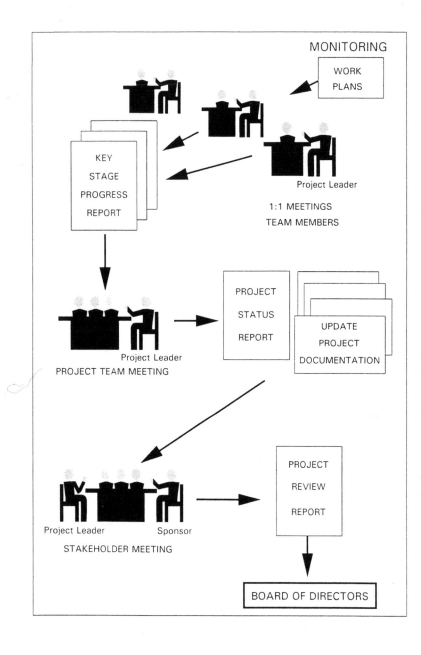

Fig. 6.1 Meetings Relate to the Reporting Process

experience for everyone. It is essential for you to set out some ground rules from the beginning to demonstrate that meetings are to serve a specific purpose and not present people with an opportunity to abdicate their responsibilities.

The project management process is time specific and you can easily get trapped into wasting the most valuable resource you have available. You have established a procedure for reporting progress and the project status. There is clearly a link between reports and these meetings, each complementing the other, so meetings should not be seen as an opportunity for repeating what everyone has already read for themselves – if they have bothered to read the reports! It is useful to establish these links as part of your project methodology so that the stakeholders and team members understand when to expect reports. An example is shown in Figure 6.1.

Regular 1:1 meetings

Through monitoring you have a good understanding of what is happening as the project progresses. Although you have informal dialogue with team members at intervals it is important to have a more formalised meeting at least once every four weeks with each individual working in the project team. The frequency may justifiably be greater for transient team members or those who join the team for just a few weeks.

These meetings which you limit to a maximum of one hour duration are best scheduled from the start of the project so that everyone knows in advance when to meet with you and discuss their progress. The meetings serve a number of fundamental purposes:

- Review action points from previous meeting
- Updating yourself on progress of their work
- Discussing any existing problems and giving guidance
- Anticipating potential difficulties ahead
- Assessing forecasts to completion of their current work plan
- Assessing their other commitments and priorities
- Reviewing their performance with the current work
- Reviewing any identified training needs and how to satisfy these
- Reviewing their capacity for future work plans in the project
- Understanding their aspirations and motivational needs
- Exposing any relationship problems that exist with others
- Any personal grievances

This is not a comprehensive, exclusive list of topics but most are relevant to your relationship with each member of the team. A key element of effective teamwork is the task of getting to know your team members. Through this understanding you are able to fully utilise the skills available to you for the benefit of the project. At the same time you can constructively help your team motivation and individual development through the experiences gained working for you on the project. This type of meeting does not need a formal agenda, but rather a general structure to ensure that anything that needs discussion is not ignored. You must record the key action points in your **project diary** and follow up the meeting with a written summary record to the individual.

These 1:1 meetings are important and you must ensure the team do not regard them as something to avoid or postpone at will or just request when a crisis hits the project. One of the reasons for holding the meetings is to minimise fire-fighting through good anticipation of potential risks and problems.

Project team meetings

Everyone accepts that involvement in a project team means they must attend project meetings. Unfortunately there is a wide range of opinions and confusion about what format such meetings take, what is discussed, who attends and what happens consequently. There is even an opinion often voiced that 'there is little point in holding a meeting when there is nothing to discuss.' Nothing could be further from reality since the co-ordination of the project work and progress is brought into sharp focus with regular project team meetings. Calling the project team together for a meeting only when a crisis hits is more likely to generate conflict and a search for where (and upon whom) to place blame than yield constructive action planning to limit the damage and keep the project on track.

Why do meetings fail?

Why do project meetings always seem to have a reputation? Is it because they do not appear to achieve very much because the real decisions are made outside the meeting? Or is it because they just seem to go on and on for hours? If either is true then something is clearly wrong and yet the meeting process itself is often diminished to a low priority. Meetings are a high cost to the organisation so you have an obligation to make them as effective as possible. Much time is wasted in waiting for meetings to start and during the meeting process. This wasted time is lost productive time on your project so do not contribute to this lowering of efficiency in the belief that you are encouraging teamworking. Many people get very frustrated by the obligation to sit in meetings when they have nothing to contribute and would much rather do something to achieve results!

Meeting failure is a perception by the members of the meeting and is frequently due to one or more primary reasons:

- **Lack of purpose**

  It is not clear why the meeting is held because of a lack of thinking about the outcomes to be achieved. Also it is important to identify if anyone other than the project team members needs to attend. Attendance for 'information purposes' is always a doubtful reason for attending a meeting, since it infers the person has to attend but does not have an opportunity to contribute.

- **Lack of planning**

  How many times have you attended a meeting that has not been planned? A project meeting must have an Agenda. It is the 'route map' to the point you hope to reach in terms of outcomes. This requires you to think about what are high priority topics that definitely need certain people to be present if you are to make and take key decisions for action. You also need to consider the timing, suitable location for the meeting and support facilities such as visual aids, meeting roles and the advance warning of the meeting.

Your earlier planning has inserted the regular project meetings into the plan, so everyone closely involved with your project will know the schedule of meetings. This does not necessarily mean you do not need to remind them, because their workload may affect their willingness to attend your project meeting – or provide them with an apparently good excuse to avoid it!

■ **Lack of control**

Control of the meeting is a fine balance between domination and a 'free for all'. A dominating chair stifles discussion and discourages active participation, usually through a strong desire to hear his or her own voice and force his or her opinions exclusively on the meeting. A 'free for all' develops in a meeting with a chair who abdicates all responsibility, allows and encourages deviation from the agenda, is unclear about the meeting purpose and does not develop clear outcomes and action plans. The chair must ensure the meeting stays on track and if interesting side issues arise during the meeting, take a decision who will deal with it, how and when – but outside the meeting.

Although these are the most common problem areas with meetings do not forget to ensure that people attending your project meetings know the ground rules. You must set the standards and tell people what you expect from them in a meeting to keep participation going but not in excess. You have experienced the chair who takes the view that the meeting "will finish when we are ready to finish, and not before". The project meeting should be carefully timed, with each topic and the duration of the whole activity. Experience will show you how much time you need but do not keep a meeting going just because others believe it should last for a minimum of three hours to demonstrate that it is achieving something. A fixed start and finish time is essential to allow everyone attending to plan their day in the interests of your project.

The meeting agenda

The project team meeting is a more formal gathering and in the interests of time and objectivity you must have a published agenda. This is probably based on a standard format including taking in the latest report from each team member. If there are specific problem areas for discussion these can then be added to the list. Check with team members in advance to see if they have any topics to be considered for inclusion in the agenda. You decide what goes in the final version. Avoid the temptation to put 'Any Other Business' at the bottom of the list – it will prolong your meeting unnecessarily and time will run away before you realise. You must decide how long the meeting should last and remember meetings are more likely to be effective at the early part of the day not the end. Set a deadline of one hour or longer if necessary (although two hours is a preferred maximum), then ensure you stick to it. You all have important work to do for the project so don't keep the team away from their work any longer than is absolutely essential.

Issue the agenda in advance of the meeting. Project work lends itself to a standard format for the progress meetings with any additional items added as necessary. A typical format for the meeting agenda is shown in Figure 6.2.

There are sometimes very recent matters that team members feel may need urgent inclusion in the agenda and warrant

PROJECT MEETING

PROJECT: SCOR
VENUE: MTG ROOM 3   START TIME: 10.30 am
DATE: 30 June   FINISH TIME: 12.30 pm
PURPOSE: Review of status and planning progress

Agenda

		Sponsor	Time - mins.
1. ACTION LIST - Report back		JF	15
2. CURRENT STATUS REPORTS			
	- Key stage 1	GH	5
	- Key stage 2	TD	5
	- Key stage 3	AP	5
3. SLIPPAGE IN KEY STAGE 3		AP	15
	Action plan decisions	JF	5
4. FORWARD PLANNING			
	- Key stage 4	TD	5
	- Key stage 5	AG	8
5. ANTICIPATED PROBLEMS AHEAD		JF	10
6. RISKS REVIEW		JS	10
7. REVIEW OF STAKEHOLDER LIST		AG	5
8. PERFORMANCE EVALUATION		JF	10
9. SUMMARY OF UPDATED ACTION LIST		TD	10
10. CLOSE			

ATTENDENCE LIST:

John Fairburn - CHAIR
Graham Hunting - TIMEKEEPER
Tony Dearburn - RECORDER
David Williams
Jennifer Scowcroft
Angela Galt   Date issued: June 24

Please attend promptly

Fig. 6.2   A Project Meeting Agenda

discussion. As you have decided to exclude the 'Any Other Business' item, open up these issues at the start of the meeting by asking all members of the team if they have any significant issues that are not on the agenda list. Within a few minutes you can then decide whether any such issues are urgent enough to include or displace a less urgent topic. Also you can take a decision about the need to involve all the team in the discussion or refer the matter for subsequent discussion after the project team meeting with just the relevant person or persons involved.

One important time-saver for project meetings is to ensure that the latest status reports are issued to everyone before the meeting, with a reminder to read through them. Make it clear that you do not want long verbal reports of progress in a meeting, repeating what is already written down. The verbal report should concentrate on briefly stating:

- What is going well
- Where problems exist with time, cost and resources
- What actions are planned to correct the problems
- What the meeting needs to debate and decide, if anything
- Any anticipated problems, risks or performance deviations

Since you have set up times for each topic as part of your meeting plan it is necessary to **appoint a timekeeper** to help you control the time. Team members will soon get accustomed to being paced and thank you for the good control you are using to avoid wasting time. Rotate the role either from meeting to meeting or even within a meeting, and as chairperson, abide by your own time decisions! You also need to **appoint a recorder** to note down the key points of discussion, particularly decisions taken, and keep a record of the **ACTION LIST**.

Using visual aids

The use of visual aids in meetings is valid depending on the need. It is unlikely that slides or viewfoils can be justified because of the preparation time required. But the flip chart is an invaluable tool. Set out the agenda topics on a sheet of flip chart paper and display this where everyone can see it. The most valuable use of the tool is in the recording of actions. Draw up a blank table of actions for the meeting **ACTION LIST** as shown in Figure 6.3. Each time there is an action decided in the meeting, it is written up on the form by the **Recorder**. Everyone in the meeting can see who is going to do what is decided and by when. This builds involvement, acceptance and commitment and there is no excuse for not knowing what is happening. It is a simple task to then get the list typed after the meeting and issued to everyone and since it is unchanged there are no surprises for anyone.

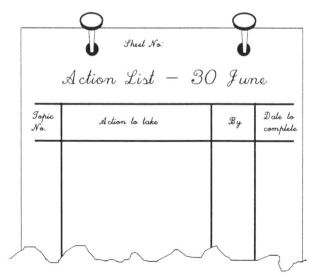

Fig. 6.3   Action List of the Flip Chart

Although you will make notes in your project diary through-out each project meeting you cannot guarantee that the team members will follow your example even with your encouragement. You may decide to issue minutes after the meeting, but wherever possible these are best confined to decisions taken and explanatory support of the action list rather than a verbatim record of the meeting. Where you have meetings with external stakeholders then you need to confirm in writing what happened and what decisions were taken in the meeting. Such meetings often require the use of influence and persuasion skills to get what you believe is right for the project.

Negotiation meetings

In project work there are two fundamental types of negotiation meetings:

■ With external stakeholders – suppliers, consultants etc
■ With other functional managers internally

The former type usually involves some form of contract that is usually subject to legal status. This requires specialist knowledge that you may have to either acquire yourself or seek from a supporting colleague or consultant. If you do not have an understanding of contract law, then it is prudent to seek advice and support before entering into purchase and supply contracts. Usually this skill is in the organisation in the purchasing function and you can make full use of their support. You will also find most purchasing experts will have developed considerable skill in the negotiating process, particularly with reference to getting such parameters as cost and time favourably agreed. You can then confidently confine your input to such meetings to ensuring that the technical details are correct and specifications satisfied.

In executing your project you are always faced with the need to negotiate with colleagues, other managers and the key stakeholders. Negotiation is essentially:

the process to resolve a situation where two or more parties have apparently incompatible objectives and where each party can, to some extent, block the other's achievement of his or her objectives.

You are faced with securing support from stakeholders and obtaining resources from other functional areas of the organisation and your skill in this process is a key factor in achieving success. When you ask for tangible support you are interfering with someone else's workload, priorities and even motivation. You must persuade them of the need and the benefits that can ensue for you as well as their department or even them, through personal development. So you start from a position of conflict and although your objective is to get a package of work done for your project, do not forget that your primary objective is to resolve the underlying conflict you provoke with your request.

Using your authority

Clearly your authority is relevant in negotiating, since power plays a significant role in the process as shown in Figure 6.4.

If you have high authority, then you are in a position to demand. You want willing co-operation so acting 'heavy handed' is not likely to produce high levels of motivation and high performance.

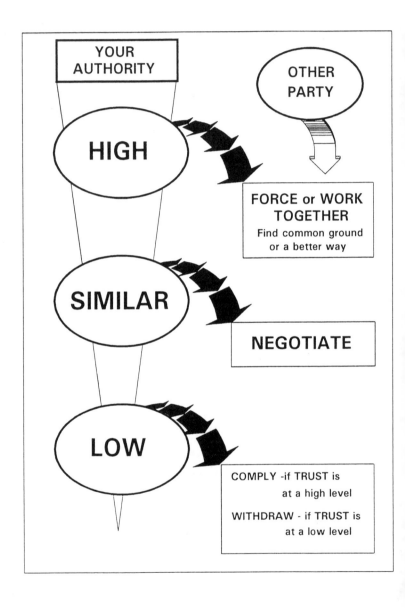

Fig. 6.4   Authority and Negotiation

If you have similar authority to the person you are negotiating with, then the process is dominated more by time and the level of trust that exists between you. This is the area where true negotiation takes place since all the parties are seeking to 'win' and get the outcomes each desires. You are striving to achieve a **win – win** result where everyone can feel a sense of satisfaction with the outcomes agreed.

The same is also true if the negotiation is with someone with low authority, but you are unlikely to have a successful negotiation since compliance [both willing or unwilling] is the almost certain outcome in most situations at work. There is no certainty of co-operation however, because the imposed outcome may give rise to feelings of dissatisfaction.

Clearly there are sound reasons for ensuring you have well defined authority as the project leader.

Seeking a 'win – win' outcome

You normally enter into a negotiating situation to secure the availability of resources for your project, either by direct assignment to your team or as a service to the project. In either situation you need to 'win' and so does the other party for a successful outcome. If you 'win', i.e. get what you want from the discussions, but the other party considers they have 'lost' through having to revise their priorities and/or objectives, you may have created a downstream problem for yourself. Many 'win – lose' outcomes degenerate to 'lose – lose' outcomes eventually, since the 'losing' party will seek an opportunity for obvious or subtle revenge and payback. All your efforts must concentrate on achieving the elusive 'win – win' outcome and this may require calm patience and full use of your inter-personal skills.

Always remember your primary objective – achieving the project objectives. This is something you have to sell to others, who may see your negotiations as a means to another end and one that is potentially harmful to them! Of course you are not seeking to exercise power over others really, but your actions are easily misinterpreted if they have any feelings of insecurity in the discussions with you. Setting yourself high targets is an essential step for you, but exposing these at the wrong moment can seriously hinder your chances of an acceptable outcome and raise the possibility of a deadlock.

A checklist for negotiation

Every situation is different so there is no simple checklist that is universally applicable. However every negotiation with other managers will have a common underlying focus, the success of the organisation. Use the checklist of Figure 6.5 as a basis for creating your own that is appropriate in your organisation.

Like every other activity in which you engage, planning is a key element to your future success. Your lack of preparation is likely to create an impression of uncertainty and lack of confidence that enhances the possibility of the other party feeling he or she will get what he or she wants and you will fail to achieve your objectives. Through careful planning you can decide your approach tactics so that you enhance the relationship rather than damage it for the future. You may need help again with the project work.

NEGOTIATION - A SHORT CHECKLIST

PREPARATION
1. Clarify what you are negotiating about
2. Identify the issues other party will raise
3. Determine their knowledge of you and your needs
4. Identify the strengths and weaknesses of other party
5. Identify their most likely objections to your requests
6. Write down your ideal settlement
7. Identify the worst you will agree to accept
8. Identify the arguments to support your case
9. Determine the benefits you can offer other party
10. Ask what unpleasant consequences they may suffer
11. Identify objections to these consequences
12. Ask what are the weak points of my case
13. Check how other party behaved in other negotiations
14. Identify if you can do anything now to strengthen your hand

BARGAINING
15. Open by asking for more than you expect to get
16. Let other party talk - you listen actively
17. Stress the importance of your project to the organisation
18. Ask questions to determine their position
19. Don't accept a first offer
20. Never offer more than you have power to give
21. Do not give way to impulses
22. Consider all implications before accepting a concession
23. Avoid debating sanctions outside your power or control
24. Remain firm and assertive, but always calm
25. Remain objective - do not be diverted to other issues

CONCLUDING
26. Summarise what is agreed and what is left in abeyance
27. Agree what issues are referred to the Sponsor - if any
28. Confirm your communication procedures to them
29. Clarify and confirm the benefits to them
30. Agree when you will meet again

DON'T:
- infer other party is unreasonable
- respond immediately to counter proposals - take time to think
- lose your temper even if they get emotional

DO:
- explain `why' you are doing something
- give reasons for disagreeing
- ask questions to clarify your understanding
- use your strongest argument on it's own - not in with others

Fig. 6.5   Checklist for Negotiating

It is also important to search for some common ground in the negotiation process. The work you need carried out may require someone to acquire new skills or further develop unused skills. This benefits you but also benefits their department for the future as well as supporting motivation driving forces. Remain cool and calm even if it takes longer than you believe is reasonable. As a last resort you can refer the matter to the **project sponsor** for arbitration, but this could lead to enmity and you are trying to reduce such a possibility not increase it.

The key to most successful negotiation with your colleague managers is your ability to listen actively, ask relevant questions and remain flexible in your approach throughout the process.

Review meetings with stakeholders

The review meetings are planned at the start of the project implementation, frequently timed to coincide with milestones in the plan. Since these milestones are significant points in the project where you have identified measurement of the success, factors can be assessed for progress towards the project objectives.

Most of the skills you employ in other types of meetings are also relevant to these review meetings. However it is important to remember the purpose of these meetings. The review is your direct means of informing the stakeholders of the status of the project at the time. It is also an opportunity for you to reinforce the need for their continued support. In return you must demonstrate that you are making a concerted effort with your team to meet their expectations from the project. In short you want them on your side, not in conflict with you. You must seek to convince them with careful arguments when changes to the plan or even the objectives appear to be necessary. Similarly when they demand changes you must remain flexible and positive, offering constructive reasons for your disagreement when it occurs. After all your efforts to launch the project, your team will expect you to avoid late changes that may seriously affect progress or alter the direction of the work. Yet your obligation [and theirs, you remind them] is to the project and you need to accept changes graciously but be aware of the potential consequences. If you have planned carefully, assessed potential risks regularly and derived contingency plans for suspect or uncertain areas, then you will not be too surprised when something unexpected happens.

If you believe modifications to the plans or objectives are necessary then prepare your case carefully. The stakeholder review is likely to be a formal meeting and demands a high standard of professional presentation from you with carefully prepared reports and charts showing progress. Expect your process management skills to be tested and examined under questioning. Demonstrate that you are in control of the project process and have established effective procedures that are working in practice.

If you plan to ask one or more stakeholders to do something for the project, do some fact finding before the meeting to ensure that your request has a reasonable chance of acceptance. Do not spring surprises at the meeting; it may create a negative response and not help you achieve your objectives.

This is particularly relevant when you need their support to arbitrate in resource conflict problems or support you in negotiations with external stakeholders.

Meeting the steering group

Occasionally it may be necessary for you to present the project status to the **Project Steering group**. This may cause you to feel concerned when you are asked to attend such a meeting. Approach the meeting in a positive way. They are doing their job by reviewing the status of all projects in the organisation to ensure they are:

- all still relevant to the organisation's corporate plan
- all still of strategic importance
- assessing and if appropriate, adjusting priorities of all projects
- verifying your project continues to progress in the right direction

Provided you are confident that you are in control of your project the only concern you need have is that your project may end up with a modified priority. If this is raised your project assumes a new level of importance that may give you additional authority. But the priority may be reduced for organisational reasons. This is not a reflection on your performance but merely reflects the organisation's re-assessment of current needs. Any decision made to put a project into a 'hold' status is never taken lightly since the cost in people's time has already been accumulated.

All meetings in project work are a direct cost on the project. You can keep costs down by careful attention to a few simple rules to make your meetings professional, effective and interesting.

Summary

- Establish a regular pattern of 1:1 meetings with your team
- Ensure that performance is a high profile topic of concern
- Hold regular project team meetings
- Ensure that your meetings are well organised and structured
- Monitor progress of all Action Plans
- Prepare carefully when entering negotiation meetings
- Always seek to obtain win – win outcomes
- Keep review meetings with stakeholders objective

7

Problem Solving

All project work is laced with problems. It is an intrinsic characteristic of the process of change that problems will surface from time to time. You can expect them, so regard them as an opportunity with a challenge. Unfortunately you rarely see the whole problem – only the 'tip of the iceberg'. Perception is relied on to show the existence or development of a problem, but this does not help you determine the underlying causes. You are confronted with the symptoms apparent to everyone, but you cannot see below the surface – see Figure 7.1.

You or your team members may believe you know the answer to a particular problem because you have 'seen it all before'. But if this statement is true then you have probably only reacted to symptoms and not treated the causes. If you had the problem would not have recurred! Anyway you are not going to fall into the trap of believing a problem perceived as recurring is necessarily the same

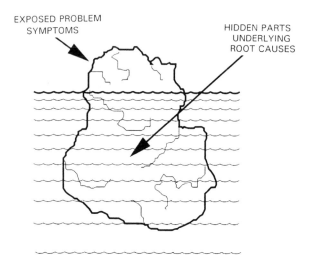

EXPOSED PROBLEM
SYMPTOMS

HIDDEN PARTS
UNDERLYING
ROOT CAUSES

Fig. 7.1   Root Causes under the Symptoms

exactly as previously. It never is quite the same so the
solution options are unlikely to be the same. Approach
each problem in a constructive and systematic way and
you can expect lasting solutions.

Diving below the surface

To establish the true scope of the problem you must go
hunting for information to describe the size and shape of
the hidden parts. Having sought and agreed the team's
views of what it is that constitutes a problem you can then
proceed to the next essential step – **fact finding**. This is
a process of data collection through asking questions to
elicit as much background information as possible. This
step is frequently ignored because of an assumption that
the cause is already 'well known' or in the interests of
time utilisation. The team's 'expert' is asked for a way
out of the problem and it is clearly a potential risk to take
the first opinion expressed under the guise of expertise.

This is not to denigrate the 'expert', since it may later turn out to be the best solution, but at least you have increased your confidence level if you use a more rigorous process. A typical list of questions for fact finding is given in Appendix 1.

Having collected as much data as possible about the problem you are ready to analyse the information to derive the most probable cause or causes. There are several techniques used in problem solving for cause analysis:

- brainstorming
- repetitive WHY – WHY diagram
- cause and effect diagrams

The first of these is a technique you use for various activities, even planning and it is a powerful tool for problem solving either individually or in teams. There are many variations of the method in current use and you must employ the technique in a way with which you are comfortable. Do remember to suspend all judgement during a brainstorming session. Critical assessment of ideas during a brainstorming activity is the guaranteed way to kill all creativity and lateral thinking. When the group appears to reach a 'dry-out' condition you can decide:

- to adjourn the session for 24 hours
- throw in a ridiculous idea to revive lateral thinking
- select a random word from a dictionary to change thinking 'gear'
- agree you think you have enough ideas exposed

You can then proceed to analyse the ideas with clustering and development of alternatives. This helps you to decide whether further fact-finding is necessary before you take a decision.

The 'WHY – WHY' diagram

This is an extension of brainstorming into a structured, more formalised approach. It is useful for individual problem solving and you can ask each member of your team to carry out the activity alone. Then call the team together and hybridise and discuss the results.

The **WHY – WHY** diagram is derived by repeatedly asking the question: "Why does something happen?" or "Why is it a problem?" in response to a perceived effect. Having derived several possible causes from the first question, each of these in turn is then subjected to the same question to give further causes. By laying out the primary, secondary and tertiary causes in the form of a hierarchical structure chart, you can produce a diagram that shows all the possible causes of the problem effects originally observed. Through a process of analysis and judgement you can then proceed to identify more accurately all the most likely causes of the problem. An example **WHY – WHY diagram** is shown in Figure 7.2.

The cause and effect diagram

One of the most popular techniques for cause and effect analysis is the 'fishbone diagram', so called because of its resemblance to a fish skeleton. These diagrams can get quite complex, but for most rapid problem solving it is enough to restrict the diagram to just four laterals off the main spine of the diagram. This is shown in Figure 7.3 with just four major cause areas, although in some problems further laterals for materials and stakeholders may be needed. The problem as perceived is written into the 'fish-head' box on the right of the diagram.

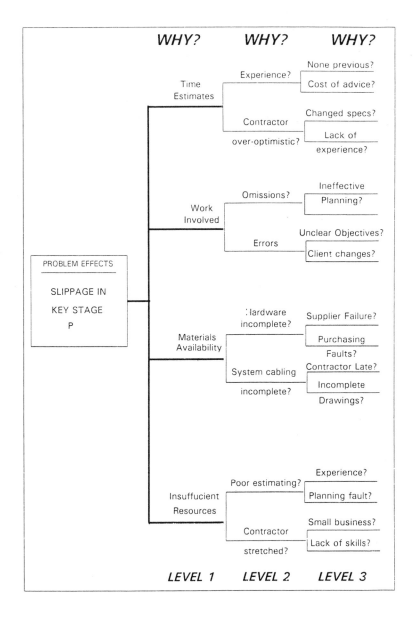

Fig. 7.2   The WHY – WHY diagram

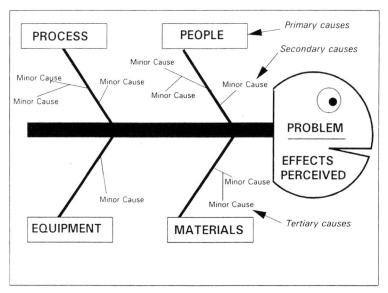

Fig. 7.3   Short form of the Cause and Effect Diagram

In a similar way to the previous technique, each lateral is examined in turn, asking some fundamental questions with respect to that particular area of the problem:

■ "Why is the effect observed?"
■ "What could be a possible cause of the problem as perceived?"

Inevitably when asking such questions, many answers have consequential questions and in this way you can identify many possible causes or factors contributing to the perceived effect. When all the possible causes are identified you can then analyse the diagram. Look particularly for factors that appear more than once or those that are closely related, even though they appear on different laterals. These are very likely to be important factors to examine as root causes of the problem and usually turn out to be different from those originally thought to be the cause.

You do not need to restrict your diagram to the short form with four laterals. It is probable that the first causes identified in brainstorming the problem are the **major causes** and these are the laterals for the diagram. Then examine each lateral in turn. The step by step process is shown in Figure 7.4.

Cause and effect analysis can be conducted by one person or as a team activity. The latter is preferred as it reinforces your teambuilding and through the involvement, creates ownership and team commitment to resolving the problem effectively and then implementing the consequent action plans.

The problem statement

When you and your team are satisfied you have clearly identified and agreed the root causes, you can revise the **problem statement** to accurately reflect your new information. This statement can now record not just the problem as perceived but list out the most probable causes that you believe are underlying the perceived effects, i.e.

The problem as perceived is................................
which we believe to be caused by one or more of
the following causes:....................................

You are now ready to proceed to generating some possible solutions to the problem. This takes you back to using simple brainstorming to create ideas. Remind the team that the important element of all brainstorming is initially to strive for quantity, not quality, and suspend ALL judgement and critical assessment until later. Your efforts are finally rewarded when you can say you have one or more

CONSTRUCTING A CAUSE AND EFFECT DIAGRAM

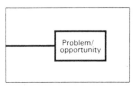

STEP 1
DEFINE THE PROBLEM/OPPORTUNITY
On a large sheet of paper, draw a box on the right hand side. This box represents the 'fish head'. Draw a horizontal line across the page to the left from the box. Write the problem effects in a few words inside the box.

STEP 2
IDENTIFY THE MAJOR CAUSES
Using brainstorming, identify each major cause and write this in a small box, above or below the main 'fishbone'. Join this box to the main fishbone with a 'rib bone'. Continue until you think you have all the major causes in place.

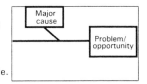

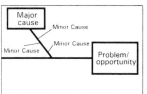

STEP 3
IDENTIFY THE MINOR CAUSES
Examine each 'rib bone' in turn, identifying the minor causes, sub-dividing as necessary. Make a separate drawing if one major cause comprises a large number of minor causes.

STEP 4
INTERPRET THE DIAGRAM
Ensure all minor causes have been identified. Draw a circle round the most likely causes. Draw lines between those that seem related. Focus on causes that appear more than once on the diagram, on different ribs. Examine these relationships since they may suggest further investigation.
Rewrite the problem statement with it's most likely causes listed.

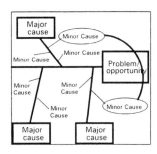

NOTES:
Major causes often fall into common categories:
People, Method, Environment, Measurement, Materials, Equipment, Management, Communications
If more than 6 or 7 major causes are identified, review the problem definition.
If the final diagram does not fully describe the problem, construct a separate diagram for each major cause as appropriate.

Fig. 7.4   Cause and Effect Diagram for Problem Solving

solutions to the problem, or at least to be accurate, solutions based on currently available information.

As the project leader you must now take the final decision which solution to adopt or if appropriate, recommend to the key stakeholders. Involving the team in this process contributes to a successful outcome. Your team's views are taken into account and you are relying on them to work with the solution and implement the subsequent action plans you are deriving in the final step of problem solving.

Action planning

Deriving action plans involves you in the consideration of:

- A strategy – what you are striving to achieve
- The tactics – how you plan to achieve the desired outcomes

The processes you have used to derive possible solutions help you to identify the desired outcomes – what you need to achieve in the interests of the project. The problem you are addressing is identified as interfering with the project process and you must ensure that the chances of recurrence are minimised. This is where you give particular attention to the tactics to employ.

One way to derive effective action plans is to develop a list of questions you must answer, starting from the point that you and the team are in agreement on the strategy. Then ask:

- Who will be affected by the solution?
- How can we best inform all those affected?
- Are there any consequential effects?

- Who will be affected by consequential effects?
- Do we need to modify the plan?
- Do we need to modify issued work plans?
- Do we need to adjust the budgets?
- Do we need to modify procedures?
- Do we need additional resources?
- Have we the appropriate skills in the team?
- Do we need outside help?
- What timescale is acceptable for implementation?
- Is the solution to be phased in?
- How can we monitor progress?
- What measurements must be made for assessment?
- When do we need to review progress?
- What indicators can we use to show further action is necessary?
- Who is responsible for implementing the action plan?

Many of these questions lead to consequential questions. In this way you can develop a comprehensive **Action Plan** that has a high confidence level for successful implementation. The key is clearly effective communication to everyone involved or affected by the implementation process, not forgetting those stakeholders who need to be informed about any changes resulting from the process.

Implementing the solution

Although your project is really itself a change process, it is often surprising that once project methods and procedures are established, it becomes difficult to make further changes to operating practices. People quickly become entrenched in the rigidity of their work practices and procedures once they are familiar. This comfortable, apparently secure position is threatened by a modification, leading to emotional behaviour and even outright opposition. You can not afford to ignore the barriers to change that can jeopardise the implementation of the **Action Plan**.

These barriers include:

■ **Cultural**
  – due to behaviours expected by the organisation, functional manager, existing traditions and customs

■ **Emotional**
  – arising from emotional needs conflicting with the solution such as anger, anxiety, feeling offended, impatience, fear of taking risks, making mistakes and the unknown

■ **Environmental**
  – distractions, expectations of others, poor communication, lack of support, boredom, stress and physical discomfort, threats to the social system at work

■ **Intellectual**
  – inability to accept methodical working, inflexible thinking, lack of knowledge or skills, threats to influence power, feeling inferior

Any of these barriers alone or collectively add up to resistance to implementing your solution and you need to be aware of the potential risks to the project. With your team examine the potential resistance you may face and take this into account in your action planning.

If appropriate call together everyone affected by the action plan to expose the implementation plan to them in detail. This allows people to question you about your decision and gives you the opportunity to create acceptance and build commitment. If new ideas suddenly surface at this meeting do not ignore them, they may be valid and help you to implement more effectively. At the same time ideas from the group, even at this stage, help to create commitment to the plan if you are seen to accept them and use them.

Summary

- Identify an initial problem statement
- Use fact finding to understand the problem better
- Use cause and effect analysis to identify underlying causes
- Derive a final problem statement
- Use brainstorming to derive alternative solutions
- Decide which option to use
- Prepare an Action Plan and identify implications
- Implement the Action Plan and communicate it effectively

8

Project Cost Control

The control of project costs is important to all organisations, but it is often not apparent at the operating level where the work is carried out. Small organisations may not have elegant control techniques but the risk of failure is high and tight monetary control is essential. The larger organisations have more control procedures, often designed for operational control but not always readily adapted to project cost control. Failure is not such a significant problem as costs are more widely spread.

As indicated earlier (see Chapter 3) control is not just confined to collecting data and analysing this for reporting. It also invokes the need for action planning to correct deviations from the plans and budgets. Cost control is not a function carried out solely by the Accounts or Finance departments, but an obligation of every member of your team throughout the project.

Most organisations have some form of **Management Information System (MIS in short)** operated by the Accounts or Finance department and project cost control is one of the sub-systems within that total system. The material inputs to that system from your project are shown in figure 8.1. Not all these inputs are always directly measured in every organisation. The cost of people's time is often the most significant cost in project work, yet it is common to find that that time is not directly measured. This is acceptable with a dedicated project team but where individuals are dividing their time between more than one project and normal operational duties, time measurement is important if effective cost control is to exist. You have established two important sets of data at the planning stage – the **approved budget** and the **operating budget** and these are the basis of your project cost control system.

The budget data is generated through the **work breakdown structure** that links directly with the project plans and schedules. This is also useful for measurement and control since it clearly describes all the work to be completed. Cost control is dependent on effective monitoring to collect the answers to some fundamental questions:

- What are the actual project costs to date?
- How do the actual costs compare with the planned costs to date?
- What work has been completed to date?
- How do the actual costs of the work completed compare with the planned costs of this amount of work?
- Based on current feedback, how much will the project cost at completion deviate from the total planned cost?

To answer these questions accurately means you must be able to link cost data directly to the **key stages** or even

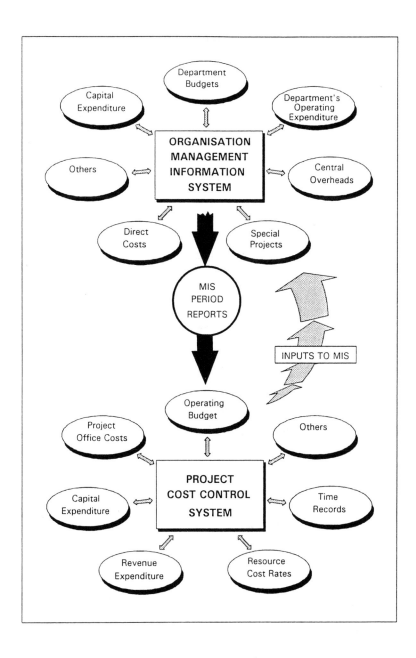

Fig. 8.1   Inputs to the Cost Control System

activities within your plan. This requires the accounting systems in the organisation to have the capability to work with activity account codes and assign incurred costs to them as they occur. This form of **activity accounting** is different to many cost accounting procedures and hence the MIS has a problem in giving you meaningful outputs. You need to apply cost data in the same way you have applied time data to individual activities for effective control.

A further problem exists in most organisations not familiar with project work. You have planned your work in considerable detail and developed an operating budget on this foundation. The management frequently do not go into operating costs in such detail unless there is a real need to investigate for some other reason. The MIS is designed to output data in collected modules as cost types by department without too much detail broken out for examination. In fact with many MIS systems it is quite a labour to generate the detail so the Finance department will do their best to discourage such detailed investigations! Among the detail you need is a report of commitments made during the period under consideration. Yet many organisations do not use commitment accounting, only recording a cost when the invoice arrives on the desk. This may satisfy accounting principles but it does not satisfy your needs for effective budget control.

Each functional area of the organisation will have account codes with sub- codes for each cost in their operation that are common for all departments. When your project is approved an account code is issued for the total project costs to enable accounts to charge all associated costs to your project. This process takes place when a cost is entered into the account ledger system. It does not take account of the cost of an individual's time unless timesheets are used by everyone as standard practice. Measuring time is often seen as a laborious, time consuming and labour intensive activity which is why it is not done. Yet many more organisations are again adopting procedures for time recording on projects, having realised that cost control is related to performance measurement. Certainly the control of a project is more difficult without these records and the organisation loses an opportunity to seek improvements in performance in the future. A potential databank of information for estimating in the future is a significant loss to everyone involved in project work.

Monitoring project costs

Monitoring of costs as they are incurred is an essential activity for you to maintain control. If investigation shows that the MIS can not provide you with the detailed support you consider you need, then you must establish your own recording system and formats. If you have access to a Personal Computer and a spreadsheet programme, it is relatively easy to set up your own record sheets and update these regularly with accurate information. It is important to recognise that if you create too much paperwork for team members to complete, you risk a reduction of motivation. Get the team involved in designing your own simple system. Their involvement builds ownership and commitment to make it work, since they do have a vested interest in a successful project.

All cost monitoring is aimed towards deriving the variances to the budget to enable you to take corrective action if necessary.

Value of the work performed

The control system is essentially seeking out variances. To support this search for cost variance you need to use some key cost measures:

ACTUAL COST OF THE WORK PERFORMED [ACWP]

The actual amount expended, including commitments, in completing the work completed within the period under consideration.

BUDGETED COST OF THE WORK PERFORMED [BCWP]

The budgeted cost for the work completed in the period under consideration, including support and allocated overheads.

BUDGETED COSTS OF THE WORK SCHEDULED [BCWS]

The budgeted amount for the total work scheduled, according to the plan, to be completed in the period under consideration, including support and overheads.

For all these key factors the period starts from project start date to the date of measurement, i.e. cumulative costs. The **BCWP** is sometimes referred to as **the earned value of the work achieved.** Collecting cost data on a regular basis allows you to generate these key factors and plot the **cost control diagram** shown in Figure 8.2. This gives you, your team and the stakeholders an instant and graphic view of the status of your project at any point in time.

In fact it is worth plotting this diagram on a large sheet and displaying it in the office continually. If you are ahead of budget then it motivates the team as they perceive success is in sight. If you are in an adverse situation it motivates the

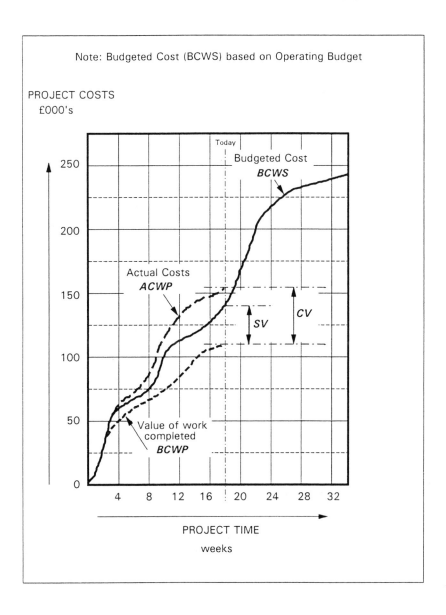

Fig. 8.2   The Cost Control Diagram

team to improve their performance to bring the project back on track, avoiding being associated with an ailing project.

Measuring the variances

The data generated for the cost control diagram yields the data for calculation of variances – the cost variance and the schedule variance:

$$\text{Cost Variance} = \text{BCWP} - \text{ACWP} = \text{CV}$$
$$\text{Schedule Variance} = \text{BCWP} - \text{BCWS} = \text{SV}$$

The schedule variance is a useful measurement because it provides an integrated indication of cost and time against a common baseline. These two variances are shown on Figure 8.2. A negative Cost variance indicates a cost over-run condition developing and a negative Schedule Variance indicates your project is running behind schedule.

These variances are also sometimes quoted in percentage terms:

$$\text{Cost Variance \%} = \text{CV} / \text{BCWP}$$
$$\text{Schedule Variance \%} = \text{SV} / \text{BCWS}$$

The units for the Schedule variance can be time in hours, days, weeks or in cash as pounds, hundreds or thousands of pounds. You must ensure that consistent units are used by everyone. The Cost Over-run at any point can be calculated from:

$$\text{\% Cost Over-run} = [(\text{ACWP}) - (\text{BCWP})] / (\text{BCWP})$$

A negative value indicates a cost under-run. The period by period value can also be plotted graphically to show the project status to date as shown in Figure 8.3. along with the cumulative schedule performance.

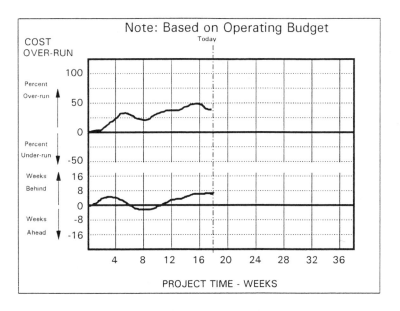

Fig. 8.3   Cost and Time Cumulative Curves

Although these factors and cost formula are applicable to the cumulative position of the project at any time, they are equally applicable to individual key stages. Then your status reports can give a detailed analysis of the financial position with your project as shown in Figure 8.4.

This is quite useful when you have assigned a key stage of your project to one department. You can allocate cost control responsibility also to the departmental representative on your team. If you can get cost data analysed at primary planning level it gives you valuable data for the future and other projects, enhancing confidence levels in estimating and costing.

Deriving the data period by period outside the MIS gives you a direct comparison with the Finance department view

COST CONTROL REPORT		Project: EFTAB Date: 28/6/93 Period: 6							
KEY	Status	BCWS		BCWP		ACWP		VARIANCE %	
STAGE No.		This Period	To Date	This Period	To Date	This Period	To Date	SVP	CVP
1	C	4	10	4	10	4	10	0	0
2	C	1	5	1	5	1	5	0	0
3	C	1	5	1	5	2	6	0	-20
4	S	3	4	2.5	3	3	3.5	-25	-16.7
5	NS	0	8	0	0	0	0	-100	-
6	NS	0	23	0	0	0	0	-100	-
7	S	3	6	3	3	2	2	-50	33
total		12	61	11.5	26	12	26.5	-57	-1.9
ALL COSTS IN £000'S									

Notes:
1. All variances based on cumulative `To Date' figures
2. Costs running at 1.9% over budget due to higher overtime costs
3. A high `Behind Schedule' figure is due to the late start of key stages 5 & 6
4. Estimate at completion = (26.5/26) X 61 = £62,200
5. The slippage of Key stages 5 & 6 will increase labour cost by £3,400

Fig. 8.4   Cost Control Report

and you can compare and validate the reports. By taking the period results for the above factors as well as the cumulative view, you can also analyse trends in performance for your project. Cost control is never easy since there are so many opportunities for others to charge costs to your account code and you must keep an alert eye on th MIS reports to ensure you are not being charged incorrectly. With careful attention to detail you can enhance your confidence of achieving project success – meeting the project objectives on time and within budget.

Summary

Ensure your budget data is updated and accepted
- Decide the key inputs to your control system
- Decide how all costs are to be measured
- Communicate the measurement methods to all team members
- Set up your own recording system
- Start a cost control diagram
- Derive an appropriate cost control report format

9

Trade-Offs in Control

Leading a project team to achieve project objectives is a complex role as you have realised. This is not made any easier by the intricate balancing act you must perform with the essential elements of resources, time, cost and performance. Achieving the right results and performance in the planned time and at the budgeted cost is the ideal and can be realised if everything flows smoothly throughout the project life cycle. Unfortunately life is not so simple for you and the inevitable crisis is always just around the next corner! The resulting upset to the balance of the four essential elements leads you to make decisions where you must make some trade-offs between these elements to maintain project integrity and progress. Then there is a deviation to one or more of these elements from the planned condition as shown in Figure 9.1.

The trade-offs available to you are subject to the project constraints you have at the time. You may be faced with

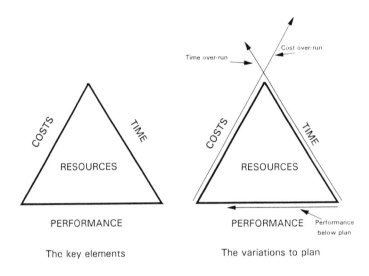

Fig. 9.1   The Elements for Trade-Offs

any one of time, cost and performance being fixed, leaving the remaining two as variable. Alternatively you may have a situation where any two of the three elements are fixed. It is quite likely that time is a fixed constraint – the project objectives must be achieved by a fixed date. Cost constraint always exists, but a cost contingency does exist up to a certain agreed amount and you can apply to use this if special circumstances exist. Performance is nearly always variable because it is primarily dependent on the people involved in the project. If the right skills are not available then you must seek to acquire them within the constraint of cost. Clearly it is not always possible to sacrifice one element without affecting another.

Numerous factors influence you in making trade-offs:

- Availability of resources
- Changes to corporate needs
- Revisions to corporate strategy

- Changes to the market place
- Customer expectations

Developing trade-offs is similar to problem solving since you are faced with examining several alternative courses of action in the interests of the project and then balancing these with the external influences. During the problem solving process various options for resolving the problem are derived and one or more of these are certain to demand a trade-off.

You have established the cause of the problem using the techniques of Chapter 7 and the next step is to review the project objectives with your key stakeholders. If there is no hope of flexibility here (as is often the case), then you are faced with a detailed review of the project environment and current status with respect to times, costs and performance measurement. If your organisation is quality conscious you will be reluctant to compromise performance. You must then examine the project context with your sponsor to determine if there is any change of priority for the organisation. There may be a downstream effect on other functional managers who have been given new priorities putting your project further down the list. Possibly the organisation is taking on too many projects concurrently and stretching resources to the point where performance suffers or time and hence cost has lost its importance in favour of 'getting results'.

Finally you must review your detailed planning for the present and forward work plans to establish updated information on:

- The time to complete the project
- The cost to complete the project
- The amount of work outstanding and resources required

Having satisfied yourself you have accurate updated information you can then look for the alternatives available to you. This requires you to derive the answers to some specific questions with your team on each of the elements.

PERFORMANCE

- Are the original standards and specifications negotiable?
- Can we still meet the original requirements?
- If not, what is the cost of compliance?
- Are there any benefits to changing the standards?
- Are there serious consequences to the organisation of dropping standards?
- What is the customer's attitude to such changes?
- Are we performing effectively now?
- If not, what actions can we take to improve performance?
- If we can, what is the consequence in terms of time and cost?
- Will a change cause us to lose resources?
- Will this loss compromise the rest of the team?

CURRENT SCHEDULE TIMES

- What is the current forecast of total project slippage?
- Is this delay acceptable to the key stakeholders?
- Will this delay affect other projects operating now?
- Will the delay cause delay of new projects?
- Are we clear why there is a slippage?
- What can be done to reduce slippage without extra resources?
- Is additional time likely to improve performance?
- If not, why not?
- Can the customer accept a time delay?

- Can the customer accept a re-phasing of outcomes?
- What is the cost of a revised schedule, including re-planning?
- Can we quantify the cost effect of delay for the business?
- Is this significant?
- Will the delay affect our reputation externally?

COST DATA COMPARED TO THE OPERATING BUDGET

- What has caused costs to over-run the budgets?
- Can the cost to completion be reduced?
- Will cost reduction affect the outcomes and quality?
- Will the customer accept the increased cost?
- Can we offer extra benefits in return for increased costs?
- Can we absorb the increased costs within contingency limits?
- Will the sponsor support an application for additional funding?
- Are we sure our budgets are still accurate?
- Is increased cost the only way to achieve the right results?
- Can we forfeit time and performance to keep costs in budget?
- Is the schedule so tight that increased costs are inevitable?
- Are we sure our estimates and schedules are accurate?

You will probably think of some other questions to add to this list for your trade-off analysis and when you have generated the answers you can start the process of decision taking. Based on which constraint is fixed, you must attempt to derive an action plan to resolve the problem.

It is appropriate to derive more than one option to present to your key stakeholders, particularly if you have two variable elements. If all three elements are fixed then you have little scope available to you. With the other combinations of the elements fixed and variable you must derive realistic options that you can demonstrate have been critically assessed with your team. It is a common mistake in making trade-off decisions to concern yourself only with the project. Remember that the external factors must be taken into account, especially the effect on current business and reputation.

Often the scope for trade-offs is limited and your options reduce to a short list of possibles, for example:

- Review the **work breakdown structure** – even down a further level
- Reduce scope and standards for non-critical activities
- Reallocate the resources available to you
- Set a minimum performance standard for critical and non-critical activities remaining
- Review, and reduce where possible, all data gathering procedures
- Reduce time consuming project documentation to a minimum
- Use lower cost resources and materials
- Renegotiate critical performance criteria with the key stakeholders
- Retain the time schedule but accept cost overspends in some areas
- Keep within the operating budget but allow slippage of the schedule and possibly also performance and quality
- Cancel the project or reduce the objectives and scope

It is possible for you to derive a checklist of possible trade-offs to use within your organisation knowing management priorities and attitudes. Although other options appear sometimes you can have some immediate options pre-planned as contingencies if certain risks or events occur. In this way you are managing pro-actively and demonstrating you are in control of the project process.

Finally of course you must get the **key stakeholders** or even the **Project Steering Group** to approve your action plans to deal with the problem and sign off acceptance of the consequences of making the trade-offs you recommend.

Summary

- Identify the fixed and variable elements for each trade-off problem
- Use brainstorming technique to establish available options
- Ask appropriate questions to establish consequences of options
- Draw up a checklist of possible actions
- Draw up your Action Plan and get it accepted by stakeholders

10

Project Termination

The day will surely arrive when you can see the end of your project in view. You have taken your team through all the crises and difficulties and had your disagreements and conflicts with them and the stakeholders. But now you are on the home straight and everything appears to be going smoothly. You may still feel concerned that some project objectives have been reduced in scope to meet the time schedules. But you can take reassurance that the sponsor has expressed satisfaction with your performance to date. However this is not the time to relax your control as there is much to consider in the run-down period. Clearly establish a **declared project finish date** and advertise it. Allowing your project to drift at the end is a sure way of escalating costs and allowing extra work to be imposed on you.

Post-project activities

Before you can sign off project completion you must ensure there is a careful consideration of all follow-up activities needed when the project outcomes are completely delivered. This will obviously depend on the type of project and the project objectives you have succeeded in delivering or will deliver at the finish date. There are few projects that have a simple clear-cut handover to the customer so this process must be carefully planned. Your intimate involvement with the project all the way through the life cycle ensures that you can determine what the handover involves and what post-project activities are necessary.

These could include:

- Establishing a small advisory/support team for a defined period
- Ensuring that adequate arrangements or contracts are made for equipment maintenance if appropriate
- Setting up training programmes for user groups
- Training trainers for future user support
- Proposing further projects to support the objectives achieved
- Preparing a post-project report

You must ensure that there are no untidy ends of work to be completed and don't allow yourself to accept additional work that is not part of the plan. There is always a temptation to get a 'few other things looked at' while you still have the team together. Remember you have not included this in the project plan so it could seriously upset your time and cost schedules if you accept extra work at this late stage. The stakeholders are unlikely to accept changes at such a late stage of the project unless they are directly related to the original objectives.

The handover

The handover process is part of the project plan and schedule. Do not regard this as something that will just happen, because it is a major pitfall area for all project leaders. Handover must be planned well in advance and started well before the **project declared finish date**. Ask the customer to nominate a small group of users as the **handover acceptance team** as early as possible, particularly if the project outcomes are delivered in a phased manner. Their role is clearly to learn about the outcomes of the project and how they are to be used and put into operational practice. You or one of your team is nominated as adviser to this team to assist them to prepare for taking over responsibility for the project results. Assist them to set up clear objectives for their implementation process – this is a further project in itself. Careful planning of the handover process, step by step, is essential to minimising conflict with your team who are completing project work. They will tend to regard the need to interact with the **handover acceptance team** as an interference with their work to complete the project on time. Tension will rise if there is any criticism of the project team's work which is quite possible as the new team becomes increasingly aware of the project outcomes. You must exercise your skills as a communicator and diplomat to get through this period smoothly! Difficulties can develop in this period as the user team starts asking questions, especially if there is any suggestion that the work of your team is suspect – not giving the exact outcomes the user team expects to receive.

You must tactfully remind them that their management as customer and a key stakeholder has accepted the work of the project team. You can assist them as much as possible but only within the constraints of time and cost imposed on the project.

Finally you must get the **handover acceptance team** to sign off the handover process at each step as it happens. This is often an area for conflict and may cause you to involve the sponsor and other stakeholders. If you have done everything the approved plan has demanded, handover acceptance cannot be unreasonably withheld.

Project evaluation

Evaluation is the process most people involved in projects will claim is an activity they do not have the time to carry out. It is an essential activity and has two modes:

- **Active evaluation – throughout the life cycle**
- **Post-project – after the declared finish date**

Both are equally important, the former being a continuous process of reviewing performance at every step of the project life cycle through the inputs to the project control system. Active evaluation is also a regular item on the agenda of project meetings (see Chapter 6).

The post-project evaluation is essential to provide data for future projects and project teams. Too often valuable experience and information is lost in project archives and never recovered for future project teams unless someone remembers – and can then find the files! Lessons learned from all aspects of project work are valuable and must be documented and distributed to all individuals in the organisation who are likely to be engaged in project work in the future. Some of the learning may be considered for inclusion in the standard project procedures in use throughout the organisation.

Post-project evaluation can concentrate conveniently on the three leadership dimensions:

- **The stakeholders**
- **The project life cycle**
- **Performance**

The process requires you to ask in-depth and searching questions with your team about each dimension. Inevitably questions lead to consequential questions which help you to establish all the key learning points from your project.

Typical consequential questions include:

1. Why did this happen?
2. What were the results?
3. Was it good or bad for the Project, Stakeholders, Team?
4. Could the situation have been anticipated?
5. Were there early signals which went unrecognised at the time?
6. When was the situation first identified?
7. Who should have reacted?
8. Was this due to unclear responsibility, authority, communication?
9. What have we learned from the event(s)?
10 How can we ensure the learning points are communicated now?

Other such questions can be added to the list for evaluation depending on specific projects, type and the team members.

Do remember to involve those transient members who may have been involved at only the early stages of the project. The purpose of evaluation is to achieve a net gain through actions. It is not an exercise in self-gratification for its own sake, so the process must be an objective one at all times.

A list of questions follows, but these are only general for all projects. You may find many others to ask about your own particular project.

TYPICAL QUESTIONS

THE STAKEHOLDERS

1. Did the project meet expectations?
2. Were the needs correctly identified initially?
3. Did the needs change during the project due to unforeseen events?
4. Were the benefits correctly identified and satisfied by the project?
5. Was the project purpose statement correct?
6. Were the expected results obtained?
7. Were unexpected results obtained?
8. Is there a follow up need to be examined in subsequent projects?
9. Were all stakeholders identified at the outset?
10 Did new stakeholders appear during the project?

THE PROJECT LIFE CYCLE

1. Was the conception carried out with leader involvement?
2. Was there a feasibility study carried out?
3. Were realistic timescales established for the project?

4. Were responsibility, authority and accountability clearly defined for the leader?
5. Were project objectives clear and understood?
6. Was there a milestone plan established?
7. Were all tasks clearly established with accurate durations?
8. Was the plan logic correct?
9. Were project resources correctly estimated?
10 Were work plans for each team member clearly established?
11 Were all team members aware of their responsibilities and authority?
12 Were milestones clearly established?
13 Were project review meetings built into the plan?
14 Were all resource constraints identified and resolved?
15 Was there a documented control system understood by everyone?
16 Were there clear lines of communication for monitoring and providing feedback?
17. How was individual performance measured and communicated?
18. Was the budget communicated to everyone?
19. Was cost and expenditure information monitored regularly & reported to the team?
20. Were the team and leader satisfied with the results?
21. Were the end users satisfied with the results?
22. Are there follow up and maintenance activities necessary?
23. What actions are required to close the project files?
24. What have we all learned from this project which will assist management in future?

THE PERFORMANCE

1. Did the team work well together?
2. Was conflict dealt with promptly?
3. Did the team and leader review their own performance regularly?
4. Have additional training needs been identified as a result of performance assessment?
5. Is recognition appropriate and necessary?

The answers you derive provide you with useful information to include in the final report to the key stakeholders. Other useful learning points derived from the experience of the project must be documented at least for the benefit of yourself and your team. Wider dissemination of such information is valid and you can discuss with your sponsor how the organisation can accept and record it.

The final report

This report is not something you do after project completion – you are then diverted to new activities and no longer have time to complete the report. Although you have delivered the project objectives the project is only really complete when this report is presented to the key stakeholders and signed off as accepted. Then you can truly celebrate!

The report should not be long and should involve all the team in its preparation to minimise the time factor. Decide on the content which should contain at least:

- Summary of objectives achieved
- Summary of project schedule
- Evidence of handover acceptance by customer
- Detailed assessment of each objective achieved

- Review of the project process (from evaluation)
- Mistakes made and corrective action taken
- Key learning points from the project
- Recommendations for further work
- Detailed information on post-project establishments
    - service, maintenance, training, support group etc

When completed, you can present the report to the key stakeholders at your final project review meeting and ask for their acceptance and sign-off, then you can go back to your team and **CELEBRATE**.

Project sign-off

Just as you launched your project with a meeting where the project was officially launched by the **Sponsor**, why not finish the project in the same way? It gives the key stakeholders an opportunity to thank the project team for all their efforts, set aside the tensions, disagreements and the general ups and downs of the project process and celebrate the success. Even if you have only partial success to record, which is only a perception anyway, it is still valid for you to hold a final meeting of everyone who has had an involvement and record the final handover of the project. It helps people to remember the successes of the project far longer than the failures!

Then you are ready for your next project assignment – or are you?

Summary

- Identify all the post-project activities required
- Ensure customer establishes a Handover Acceptance Team
- Stick to the Declared Project Finish Date
- Avoid accepting extra work not budgeted
- Set up Follow-on projects if appropriate
- Carry out a detailed post-project evaluation
- Communicate learning points identified
- Modify project methodology where appropriate
- Prepare the Final Report to Stakeholders and get it accepted

11

Looking Forward

You have now completed your project and before you move on enthusiastically to ever greater challenges, it is worth taking a little time to evaluate your own performance and gains from the experience. You have learned much from the whole process and this is part of your development and skill enhancement process. Ask yourself:

- What have you done well?
- What could you have done better?
- What further training do you need?
- What can you do to improve the project process?

This self-evaluation is a worthwhile activity to expose ways you can learn from your experience and improve your performance in the future. Present yourself with a Personal Action Plan and reward yourself each time you succeed in achieving a personal target.

Upgrade your methodology

Although many organisations are increasingly aware of the benefits of project management in achieving the desired results there is always scope for improvement in methodology and process. Identify the weaknesses and use your recent experience to influence change to achieve these improvements. Are there easier ways of smoothing the process? Can you recommend changes that benefit the organisation in total? If every project leader on every project in the organisation takes time to examine these aspects of project work, there is certain to be an improvement in performance and quality

It is easy to accept the *status quo* and hope that everything will continue to work well enough to avoid change. But projects are about change and you have an obligation to use this opportunity to make change happen on a broader front.

Using a computer

Throughout this book, mention of the use of computers in the project management process has been minimal. This is a conscious decision to concentrate on fundamental principles. Certainly there is an abundance of software available to make the task of planning and control of projects apparently easier. Much of this software is complex and takes time to learn its use as an effective tool. That is what it is – a tool and not a business game! It is easy to get trapped into spending too much time using a computer to examine alternatives, asking 'what if' type questions and examining trade-offs. Yes, it does make these tasks quicker to undertake and if the right balance is maintained then the computer is a valuable tool for planning and controlling your projects.

If you decide to use a personal computer with project management software for future projects, take time out to look at different packages and their capabilities. These programmes have a high functionality and you must determine exactly what you need the tool to do for you. If you have not used such complex programmes before, it could be a mistake to purchase a large programme that appears to do 'everything'. Many organisations have done just this and found that people do not have time to learn to use the software and lose interest when they realise its complexity. Invariably it takes a long time to learn to use the programme effectively and its use will inevitably be restricted to a select few members of the team. Select a programme that offers you the functionality you need now and graduate to something more complex later. The cost to your organisation is lower in the long term.

Undoubtedly there are project management programmes available that are relatively inexpensive and can help you to speed up planning, control and reporting of project status. These programmes make the tasks of planning changes, resource assignment and resource conflict management much easier. But do remember the computer can only do what you tell it to do for you. It is worth mentioning that most of the project documentation referred to in this book and others (see Appendix 3) can be set up as standard library reports in the programme. This ensures that all reporting for all projects follows a consistent approach in the future. This benefits everyone in the project team and the stakeholders.

The computer has a value provided you keep a sense of proportion. It can not replace the people management skills you need to control the project process. The final decisions are always left in your hands and based on your project and management experience.

Continue your development

Project management is increasingly regarded as an essential skill for managers in today's business environment. This is not strictly correct; it is much more than just a skill. It is a discipline and a professional one that puts high demands on the erstwhile student of the subject. There are many aspects to project management and hence a wide range of skills required to be effective. In reality the role of project leader embraces almost every other management skill in the organisation as well as the detailed understanding of the tools and techniques for effective planning, control and completion of projects.

Your future success depends on your commitment and dedication to developing all these skills. Success is not dependent on luck, it is 99% effort and 1% luck!

'If you don't decide your own future, someone will decide it for you'

1

Appendix 1
Fact Finding

Fact finding is the fundamental part of the process of deriving a problem statement and clear objectives for a data gathering investigation. The purpose is to collect as much known data as possible, then seek the data identified as missing to assist the investigators to derive conclusions and recommendations. The process is based on posing a whole series of relevant, accurate questions which themselves will often lead to further supplementary questions. Some examples are:

WHAT:

What is the urgency in corporate terms?
Into what parts can the problem be divided?
To what other problems does this problem relate?

What is the total situation of which this problem is part?
What is the dimension of the problem – large, medium or small?
What are the consequences of not solving the problem?
What will happen if the solution is delayed?
What are the cost effects of the problem now?
What benefits could be expected from getting a solution?
What effect has this had on other projects in operation now?

WHY:

Why did the problem appear in the first place?
Why was the problem not recognised earlier?
Why was there no attempt to find a solution earlier?
Why is it necessary to investigate the problem now?

WHEN:

When was the problem first identified?
When does the problem actually occur?
Is there any seasonal pattern to the occurrence?
When is a solution needed?
When can the data be collected?

HOW:

How did the problem come to be recognised?
How does it affect company performance and results?
How was the problem dealt with in the past?
How was it prevented from recurring previously?
How can accurate data be collected?

WHERE:

Where does the problem start?

Is the problem confined to one part of the company?

Is the problem restricted to one country or area; if so, why?

Is the problem confined to one department only?

Is the problem caused by suppliers?

Where can data best be collected from?

WHO:

Who identified the existence of the problem in the first place?

Who was responsible for its occurrence?

Who could best be made responsible for solving the problem?

Who is most affected by the problem now?

Who else might be unknowingly affected by the problem?

Who is likely to benefit from a solution?

Who can identify the consequences of the problems now?

Who is best placed to collect data on this problem?

Who should be consulted?

Collection of information is a time consuming activity, but is essential to getting the best result at the time. However hard you try there will always be information you miss. It is important that you create an open climate in the team to ensure information is not held back. It is important to ensure that people outside the team who are questioned are given clear, valid reasons for the investigation so that they can see they are not potential victims of a witch hunt!

2

Appendix 2
Glossary of Project Management Terms

There is a considerable amount of jargon used by project managers today, enhanced by the rapid growth in the use of personal computers for planning and control of projects. The list gives some of the more common terms and their usual meaning.

A

ACWP. The actual recorded cost, including costs committed, of the work actually performed up to a particular point in the project schedule.

ACCOUNTABLE EXECUTIVE. The individual, usually a

senior manager, who is held to account for the success of a project.

ACTION CYCLE. The dynamic re-iterative process of actions that a leader follows to achieve results.

ACTIVITY. A clearly defined task with known duration: often used to include a series of tasks which together complete particular step or part of the work.

ACTIVITY ON ARROW DIAGRAM. A network diagram where all activities are represented by arrows and events represented by circles.

ACTIVITY ON NODE DIAGRAM. A network diagram where all activities are represented by the node or event, usually as a box and the arrows are used merely to show the logical flow of the project.

ARROW. The symbol by which an activity is represented is represented in the Arrow Diagram.

ARROW DIAGRAM. A diagrammatic statement of the complete project by means of arrows: also known as a **Network Diagram**

B

BCWP. The budgeted cost, based on the operating budget, of the work that is actually completed up to a particular point in the project schedule.

BCWS. The budgeted cost, based on the operating budget, of the work that is planned to be completed up to a particular point in the project schedule.

BACKWARD PASS. The procedure by which the latest event times or the finish and start times for the activities of a network are determined.

BASELINE PLAN. The final 'frozen' plan as signed off by the sponsor before implementation. This is also the **Recorded**

Plan, against which all progress is measured and variances analysed and reported.

BAR CHART. A graphical presentation of the activities of a project derived from the project logic diagram shown as a timed schedule.

BUDGET VARIANCE. The analysed difference between the Approved Budget and the Operating Budget for the project, either as a project total or for each key stage.

C

CHANGE REQUEST. A standard format form to record and request approval from the key stakeholders for a significant change to the baseline plan.

CIRCLE. The symbol used to represent an event i.e. the start or finish of an activity

CONTROL SYSTEM. The procedures established at the start of the project that provides the leader with the necessary data to compare planned status with the actual status at any instant in time, to identify variances and take corrective action.

COST CONTROL DIAGRAM. A graphical representation of the actual and budgeted costs of the work actually performed against the scheduled and budgeted costs of the work planned.

COST OVER-RUN. The difference between the ACWP and the BCWP expressed as a percentage of the BCWP. A negative result indicates a cost under-run.

COST VARIANCE. The difference between the value of the work actually performed (BCWP) and the actual costs incurred and committed (ACWP)

CPM. Critical Path Method – a system where activities are represented by arrows on a diagram which can then be used for effective planning of the use of resources and subsequent control of the project.

CRITICAL PATH. The sequence of activities which determines the total time for the project. All activities on the critical path are known as **Critical Activities**

CRITICAL SUCCESS FACTORS. The factors that have a direct impact on the success of a project

D

DEPENDENCY. The basic rule of logic governing network drawing – any activity which is dependent on another must be shown to emerge from the HEAD event of the activity on which it depends.

DUMMY. A logical link, but which represents no specific operation [zero resources]

DURATION. The estimated or actual time to complete an activity

E

EARNED VALUE ANALYSIS. The process of analysing the work completed and the costs incurred to determine the value of the work completed up to a particular point in the schedule.

EET. The earliest event time – the earliest completion time for an event which does not effect the **Total Project Time**

EFT. The earliest finish time of an activity without changing total time or the spare or float time

EST. The earliest start time of an activity.

EVENT. A point in the progress of the project after total completion of all preceding activities

EXCEPTION REPORT. A standard format form for the

recording of deviations to the baseline plan, with reasons, consequences and financial implications. It is used to keep key stakeholders informed and does not necessarily automatically stop the project work.

F

FLOAT. Difference between the time necessary and the time available for an activity.
FORWARD PASS. The procedure for determining the earliest event times of a network.

G

GANTT CHART. A graphical method of showing a project schedule which shows project time, dates, all activities, resources and their relationships.

H

HARD PROJECT. A project with clearly defined objectives and readily identifiable resource requirements from the outset.
HEAD EVENT. The event at the finish of an activity. The event then changes it's nature and becomes the **Tail Event** for the succeeding activity.

K

KEY STAGE. A group of closely related activities that can be isolated together as a clear stage of the project which must be complete before passing to the next stage.

L

LET. The latest time by which an event can be achieved without affecting the Total Project Time from start to finish.
LFT. The latest possible finish time without changing the total task or float times.
LRC. The **Linear Responsibility Chart** that displays a complete listing of key stages and/or activities with the names of the resource(s) who have been allocated responsibility for each as part of the plan.
LST. The latest possible time an activity can start without affecting the total project time.

M

MIS. Management information system, normally providing at least finance and accounts information and frequently providing data for all aspects of managing a business.
MILESTONE. Another name for an event, but usually reserved for a significant or major event in the project. Often used for identifying key progress reporting points.
MONITORING. The process of checking what is happening and collecting data on project progress.
MULTI-LEVEL PLANNING. Planning the project at several levels of detail, starting with the key stages and then exploding each key stage to show all the associated activities. Where necessary any activity is further exploded to show further detail of associated tasks at the next level down and so on.
MUST DATE. A planned date when an activity or group of activities must be complete under all circumstances.

N

NODE. Another name for an event

P

PRECEDENCE DIAGRAM. A network where activity and dependency is shown by a box to represent the activity and an arrow to show the dependency link or logic. The arrows only serve to show the flow of the project between the nodes.

PREDECESSOR. The activity immediately prior to an event.

PROJECT APPROVED BUDGET. The budget approved at the conception of the project, based on outline plans only with contingency included.

PROJECT CONTROL SYSTEM. The management process and intrinsic procedures that are the basis for the systematic control of the project through the measurement and analysis of performance against the baseline plan.

PROJECT LIFE-CYCLE. A systems approach to a project where the project is described as passing through four phases from conception to termination.

PROJECT OPERATING BUDGET. The budget derived at operating level after detailed planning to first or preferably the second level is completed.

PROJECT STEERING GROUP. A senior management committee often made up of project sponsors who have the power to prioritise and steer projects in the direction necessary to meet corporate objectives.

R

RESOURCE. Anything other than time which is needed for carrying out an activity.

RESOURCE LEVELLING. Utilisation of available float within a network to ensure that resources required are appreciably constant.

RESOURCE SMOOTHING. The scheduling of activities within the limits of their total floats to minimise fluctuations in resource requirements

S

SCHEDULE. The project plan converted to 'real time' against a calendar by inserting realistic agreed time estimates and resource capacity factors into all the project activities.

SCHEDULE VARIANCE. The difference between the value of the work completed (BCWP) and the budgeted cost, from the operating-budget, of the work planned to be completed at a particular point in the schedule.

SEMI-CRITICAL PATH. That path which is next to the critical path when all paths are arranged in order of float

SLACK. Used to refer only to an event and is the latest date[time] minus the earliest date[time]

SOFT PROJECT. A project where the objectives are only broadly stated and the resources needed are unknown and flexible, the scope left open intentionally and deadlines not defined clearly.

SPONSOR. The senior manager who takes ownership of the project on behalf of the organisation.

STAKEHOLDER. Any individual who has an interest or stake in the project at any time during the project life-cycle.

SUB-CRITICAL PATH. A path which is not critical

SUCCESSOR. The activity immediately following an event.

T

TAIL EVENT. The event at the beginning of an activity

TAIL SLACK. The slack possessed by an event at the tail of an activity

TIME LIMITED SCHEDULING. The scheduling of activities such that the specified project time is not exceeded using resources to a predetermined pattern.

TOTAL FLOAT. The total float possessed by an activity

TRADE-OFF. The process of decision making and taking used in action planning to keep a project on track through identifying the best option to take between changing either cost, time, performance or resources, or combinations of these elements to maintain the project on track.

TRACKING. The process of taking progress information gathered in a control system and inserting this into the original plan to show the actual status i.e. the compliance or deviation from the planned status of the project at that point in time.

W

WORK BREAKDOWN STRUCTURE. The diagrammatic presentation of all the key stages and their associated activities arranged in a hierarchical format, showing each level of planning.

WORK PLAN. A standard format form or chart for recording an agreed listing of the tasks to be carried out by an individual or department, complete with agreed start and finish times for each within the overall project schedule.

Appendix 3
Further Reading

Critical Path Analysis and Other Project Network Techniques
Lockyer, Keith.(Pitman, London) 4th Edition 1984

Leading Projects
Young, T.L. (The Industrial Society, London) 1993

Planning Projects
Young, T.L. (The Industrial Society, London) 1993

Teambuilding
Fraser, A. & Neville, S. (The Industrial Society, London) 1993

Communication Skills – A Practical Handbook
Editor: Chrissie Wright (The Industrial Society, London) 1993

The Handbook of Communication Skills
Hurst, B. (Kogan Page Limited, London) 1991

Problem Solving Techniques that really work
Bird, M. (Judy Piatkus(Publishers) Ltd., London) 1992

Successful Problem Solving
Juniper, D.F. (W Foulsham & Co Ltd.,Slough) 1989

Systematic Problem-Solving & Decision-Making
Pokras, S. (Kogan Page Limited, London) 1989

Management Skills – A Practical Handbook (Industrial Society, London) 1993

Handbook of Management Skills
Editor: Dorothy M. Stewart (Gower Publishing Co. Ltd.) 2nd Edition 1992